Tax Strategies to Keep What You Earn

Simple Year-End Moves That Turn Tax Season Into Payday

Ignatius Nightingale

First edition, 2026

Published by Ignatius Nightingale

Contents

Chapter 1: The Refund Trap: Why You're Giving the IRS a Free Loan

Maria Rodriguez kept the refund check on her kitchen counter for three days before she deposited it. Twelve hundred dollars. She propped it against the napkin holder where she'd see it every morning—a little reminder that she'd made it through another year. She was forty-two, a home health aide in suburban Cleveland, working fifty-hour weeks.

She hadn't.

When we finally sat down to track where that money went, the story unraveled fast. Four hundred to the mechanic for a transmission repair she'd been putting off since January. Three hundred for back-to-school supplies and fees—her daughter's science camp, her son's new cleats, the lab fee the school district didn't mention until two weeks into September. Two hundred to catch up on the gas bill from a winter that had tried to kill her budget. The rest vanished into groceries and the kind of expenses you can't reconstruct afterward. Not one dollar went to anything she enjoyed. No vacation. No splurge. Not even a dinner out. She was using her own money, returned to her a year late, to patch holes that had opened up *because* she'd been running short all year.

She'd built her entire financial life around that refund. It was the silent assumption underneath every decision from May through March: *April will bail me out.* Which meant she ran tight. Really tight. Skipped the oil change. Put off the dentist. Let the credit card balance creep up, telling herself she'd knock it down when the check came. And she did knock it down—barely—before the cycle started over.

That's the refund trap, and it doesn't feel like a trap when you're in it. It feels like discipline. Like you're being responsible, living within your means, waiting for your reward. Except there's no reward. You're just getting your own money back after the government held it for twelve months, and in the meantime, every single month, you were underfunded. You could have used that money when the car started making that noise. When your kid needed new glasses. When the furnace died in January and you had to choose between fixing it and paying the electric bill on time.

I know this because I did the exact same thing. My first job out of college, I got a $3,400 refund. I was twenty-three, making $42,000 a year as a junior analyst, and that check felt like I'd won the lottery. I couldn't stop talking about it. Brought it up at lunch, mentioned it to my roommate, even called my mom to brag. Look at me. Look at all this money the government decided I deserved.

Ed overheard me. Ed was my mentor—late fifties, the kind of guy who wore the same three ties in rotation and kept a battered thermos of black coffee on his desk all day. He'd worked his way through every mistake you could make with money because he'd started with nothing and assumed that meant the rules didn't apply to him until they did, hard. He didn't say anything while I was crowing about my refund. Just waited. Let me finish my little victory lap. Then he asked me a question I can still hear in his voice: "So you loaned the government $3,400 interest-free for a year instead of putting it in your emergency fund?"

I didn't have an answer.

I stood there holding that check, and it stopped feeling like a win. It felt like evidence I'd been played. Because Ed was right. I didn't *have* an emergency fund. I'd been telling myself I'd start one as soon as things settled down, as soon as I got a raise, as soon as I paid off my car. And the whole time, I'd been sending the IRS an extra $283 a month that I could have been putting toward the exact cushion I kept saying I needed.

That conversation rewired something in me. Not immediately—I still cashed the check, and I still spent it on things I can't even remember now—but it planted a question I couldn't ignore: *What if I've been thinking about taxes completely backward?*

Because here's what nobody tells you when you're filling out your W-4 on your first day of work, still trying to figure out where the bathroom is and whether you're supposed to bring your own coffee mug: that form isn't just a bureaucratic hoop. It's an instruction set. You're telling your employer how much federal income tax to pull from every paycheck, and whatever you tell them, they do. They're not verifying it against your actual tax situation. They're not checking in six months later to see if your life changed. They just withhold what you said to withhold, and if you filled out that form five years ago when you were single with no kids and you're now married with two children and a mortgage, the withholding doesn't update itself. You're still overpaying based on who you used to be.

Most people fill out the W-4 once and never think about it again. I did that. Maria did that. Probably half the people you work with did that. And the IRS is perfectly happy with that arrangement, because overwithholding is risk-free for them. They get to hold your money all year, and then they send it back in April with no interest, and you *thank* them for it. You frame it as a win. A windfall. Something you earned by being a good taxpayer.

It's not a win. It's a symptom of a system designed to collect the maximum you'll tolerate without pushing back, and it runs on the assumption that you won't engage. Every deduction, every credit, every adjustment exists because someone fought for it—lobbied for it, wrote it into law, demanded it from their representatives—and if you don't claim it, the IRS isn't going to call you up and remind you. They'll take what you give them. If you overpay, they'll hold it and return it later. If you underpay, they'll fine you. The system doesn't care. It's structural, not personal. You have to engage, or you get the outcome designed for people who don't.

Let me tell you what that looks like in real time, because the refund trap isn't just about the money you don't have in April. It's about every decision you make between now and then.

Maria's transmission started slipping in January. Not catastrophically—just enough that she noticed it hesitating when she accelerated, a little shudder she could feel through the steering wheel. She knew what it meant. She'd owned the car long enough to recognize the warning signs. But she didn't have $400 to fix it. Not in January. Not after Christmas, not after the heating bill, not after the co-pays from her son's strep throat. So she drove it anyway. Told herself it wasn't that bad. Told herself she'd get it looked at after the refund came.

By March, it wasn't slipping anymore. It was failing. The repair bill was $1,100.

That's the cost of waiting. Not $400. Not even $700. $1,100, because a small problem turned into a big one while she was waiting for her own money to come back to her. And it's not like she was being irresponsible. She was working fifty hours a week. She was budgeting. She was doing everything right according to the logic she'd inherited from everyone around her: work hard, live within your means, wait for the refund. Except that logic has a built-in trap, and the trap is that you're always underfunded when it matters.

You're short in June when your kid's summer camp registration is due. You're short in September when school starts. You're short in November when the heat kicks on and your utility bill doubles. You're short in January when the car breaks down. And every single time, you tell yourself the same thing: *I'll deal with it when the refund comes.* Which means you're not dealing with it. You're deferring it, delaying it, letting it compound. And when the refund finally shows up, it doesn't feel like a windfall anymore. It feels like a bucket you're using to bail out a boat that's been taking on water all year.

I don't know if I can make you *feel* what that's like if you haven't lived it, but I'll try. It's the feeling of standing in the grocery store doing math in your head, putting back the name-brand cereal because the off-brand is $1.50 cheaper and you need that dollar-fifty for gas. It's the feeling of telling your daughter she can do *either* soccer *or* piano this semester, not both, because the registration fees hit at the same time and you can't cover them both until April. It's the feeling of seeing your checking account balance drop below $200 and knowing you still have a week until payday and hoping nothing unexpected comes up because if it does, you're putting it on the credit card and paying interest on your own emergency.

That's the cost. Not the $1,200 you're not getting in your paycheck every year. The cost is the stress. The cost is the decisions you make under that stress—the deferred maintenance, the delayed care, the compounding problems you can't afford to fix because you're waiting for April to save you. The cost is the interest you pay on the credit card balance you wouldn't have if you'd had an extra $100 a month to throw at it. The cost is the opportunities you miss because you don't have the cash on hand when they show up.

And here's the thing that makes it worse: the refund doesn't actually solve any of this. It just resets the cycle. You get the check, you pay down the debt, you catch up on the bills, and then you go right back to running tight for another eleven months. You never build a cushion. You never get ahead. You're just treading water, and every April, the refund pulls you back to the surface long enough to take a breath before you go under again.

I'm telling you this not to make you feel bad, but because I need you to understand what you're actually trading when you let the government hold onto your money all year. You're not trading current spending for future security. You're trading current stability for future relief, and that's a bad trade. Relief is temporary. Stability compounds.

When I finally adjusted my W-4—about six months after that conversation with Ed, because it took me that long to get over the fear of screwing it up—I didn't feel rich. I felt nervous. My take-home pay went up by $140 every two weeks, and for the first month, I kept waiting for the IRS to send me a letter saying I'd done something wrong. They didn't. The money just showed up in my paycheck, like it had always been mine, which it had.

I didn't blow it. I didn't even notice it most weeks. I'd set up an automatic transfer the same day my paycheck hit—$140 straight from checking to savings, gone before I could think about it. Within three months, I had a $1,600 buffer in my savings account. That was more than I'd ever had in my life outside of a tax refund, and this time, it wasn't earmarked for catching up. It was just *there.* Available. Ready.

The first time I used it was for something completely mundane. My laptop charger died, and instead of panicking or putting it on a credit card or waiting two weeks until payday, I just… bought a new one. Forty bucks. Ordered it online, had it two days later. And my checking account didn't implode. I didn't have to juggle anything. I just handled it, the way people with money handle things, and it was the most unremarkable, boring, life-changing experience I'd had in years.

That's what reclaiming your withholding does. It doesn't make you rich. It makes you *stable.* It gives you access to your own money when you actually need it, not when the government decides to give it back. And it forces you to think about taxes differently—not as something that happens *to* you once a year, but as something you can control, adjust, and use to your advantage.

Now, I know some of you are thinking, *What if I mess it up? What if I adjust too much and end up owing money I don't have in April?* That's a fair fear. It's the same fear I had. It's the same fear Maria had when I first suggested she update her W-4. The refund feels safe because it's guaranteed. You know it's coming. You've structured your whole year around it. The idea of giving that up—even if it means having more money every month—feels risky.

But here's what that fear misses: you're allowed to update your W-4 as many times as you want. It's not locked. If you adjust it in March and your situation changes in July—you get married, you have a kid, you take on a second job—you can adjust it again. The IRS doesn't care. They're not tracking how many times you update the form. They just withhold whatever you tell your employer to withhold.

And if you're genuinely worried about underpaying, you don't have to zero out your refund completely. Aim for a small one—$300, $500, even $700 if your situation is complicated and you want a buffer. The goal isn't perfection. It's not about hitting your tax liability to the dollar. The goal is *awareness.* It's taking the system off autopilot and putting yourself back in control.

Because the system isn't going to do this for you. The IRS isn't going to call you in February and say, "Hey, you're overwithholding—you should keep more of your paycheck." Your employer isn't going to audit your W-4 and suggest adjustments. The tax code is built to let you overpay without friction, and if you don't push back, you'll keep doing it. Not because you're irresponsible or bad with money, but because the default is designed to work against you.

Maria adjusted her W-4 in June. By July, she was seeing an extra $100 in every paycheck. The first month, she barely noticed it. It went into her account, and then it went back out to cover the usual expenses—groceries, gas, utilities. But the second month, something shifted. She had a little left over. Not much. Forty bucks, maybe fifty. She put it toward her credit card balance. The third month, she did it again. By October, she'd knocked $400 off a balance she'd been carrying for two years, and for the first time in as long as she could remember, she wasn't dreading January.

She didn't get a big refund the following April. She got $320. And she didn't miss the other $880, because she'd already spent it—on fixing the car before it broke, on paying down debt while the balance was manageable, on building a small cushion in her checking account that meant she didn't have to hold her breath every time an unexpected bill showed up.

She told me it felt like breathing room. Not wealth. Not security. Just space. The kind of space that let her say yes when her daughter's school announced a field trip, instead of having to wait and see if they could afford it after the refund came. The kind of space that meant she could buy her son the cleats he needed in August instead of making him wait until September. Small things. Unremarkable things. The kind of things that don't make a difference on paper but change everything in practice.

That's what this chapter is really about. Not tax strategy. Not deductions or credits or loopholes. It's about taking your money back from a system that's perfectly happy to hold onto it while you struggle, and using it when it actually matters—when the car starts making that noise, when your kid needs new glasses, when life throws you something you didn't budget for and you need to handle it without going into debt or waiting for April.

The refund isn't a reward. It's a red flag. It's evidence that you've been letting the system run on autopilot while you pay the cost in stress, compounding problems, and missed opportunities. And the fix isn't complicated. It's not some advanced tax maneuver that requires a CPA and a law degree. It's a form. One form, ten minutes of your time, and the willingness to see your tax refund for what it actually is.

So here's where that leaves you. You can keep doing what you've been doing—fill out the W-4 once, forget about it, let the overwithholding run on autopilot, and wait for the refund every April. That's easy. It's safe. It's what everyone around you is probably doing. Or you can pull up your most recent pay stub, look at how much federal income tax you're having withheld, and ask yourself: *Is this actually helping me, or is it just helping the IRS?*

If the answer makes you uncomfortable, there's a tool for that. The IRS has a Tax Withholding Estimator on their website. It's free. It takes about ten minutes. You answer some questions about your income, your deductions, your credits, your filing status, and it tells you whether you're overwithholding. If you are, it tells you how to fix it. And then you update your W-4, and your employer starts withholding the right amount instead of too much, and you stop giving the government an interest-free loan.

But knowing how to do it isn't the same as doing it. And doing it once isn't the same as building it into the way you think about money. The W-4 is just a form, but what it represents—what it *requires*—is a shift. You have to stop treating taxes as something that happens to you once a year and start treating them as something you manage, adjust, and control. You have to stop seeing the refund as a win and start seeing it as a warning sign. You have to be willing to engage with a system that's built to reward passivity with your own money, returned late, with nothing to show for the wait.

That shift doesn't happen because you read a chapter. It happens because you decide your money is worth more in your hands than theirs, and then you do something about it. Not someday. Not next year. Now. Today. Before another month of overwithholding disappears into a system that was never designed to give you anything you didn't fight for.

And once you've made that shift—once you've adjusted your withholding and you're keeping more of your paycheck every month—you're going to run into the next question, the one that actually determines whether any of this matters: *What do I do with it?* Because an extra hundred bucks a month isn't going to change your life if it just vanishes into groceries and gas. It only matters if you point it somewhere. If you give it a job. If you turn it into something that compounds instead of something that disappears.

That's not a tax question anymore. That's a system question. And the system—your system, the one you build to handle the money you've reclaimed—is where the real work starts.

She propped it against the napkin holder where she'd see it every morning—a little reminder that she'd made it through another year.

Maria kept the check on her counter for three days. Her mechanic wouldn't wait that long.

Chapter 2: Decoding Form W-4: Adjusting Your Withholding

You have the money. Right now. It's just not in your account. It's sitting with the IRS, accumulating in twenty-six biweekly installments, waiting for April to give it back.

Her daughter needed tubes in her ears—a routine procedure, covered by insurance, except for the $1,200 out-of-pocket portion. The scheduler called in November, pleasant but firm. They needed that money upfront or they'd have to push the surgery to after the new year when her deductible reset. Another three months of her daughter waking up screaming from ear infections.

Jennifer had the money. Technically. It was sitting with the IRS, locked into the withholding from every paycheck since January. Come April, she'd get most of it back—probably $3,000, same as every year. Her co-workers called it their "Christmas bonus." She called it her safety net. Except when she actually *needed* the safety net, it wasn't there.

She pushed the surgery to January. Her daughter was miserable through the holidays.

The National Consumer Law Center estimates that roughly seventy percent of taxpayers get refunds, and the average refund hovers around $2,800. That's $2,800 that could've been in your account, available for emergencies, earning interest, or just covering groceries during a tight month.

You might be thinking, "Yeah, but I *like* getting a refund. It's the only way I save." But here's what that "forced savings plan" actually costs you: every month you can't cover an unexpected car repair, you put it on a credit card at eighteen percent interest. Every month you can't fully fund your kid's 529 plan or your own Roth IRA, you lose out on compound growth. Meanwhile, that refund you're counting on in April is sitting in a government account doing absolutely nothing for you.

And then there's the flip side—the people who underwithhold and get slammed in April.

Kevin freelanced as a software developer on the side, pulling in maybe $15,000 a year on top of his day job. He didn't adjust his W-4 to account for that extra income. Why would he? His employer took taxes out of every paycheck; surely that covered it. Except it didn't. His side income wasn't subject to withholding at all, and when he filed his taxes, he owed $2,400. He didn't have it. So he set up a payment plan with the IRS, which came with interest and penalties that bumped the total closer to $2,700.

Both scenarios stem from the same root problem: not understanding or managing your W-4. It's one form. Five sections. And it controls whether you have access to your money or whether you're constantly scrambling.

So let's fix it.

If you owe $6,000 in federal income tax for the year, you can either have $500 taken out of every monthly paycheck—steady, predictable, manageable—or you can have $800 taken out every month and get a $2,400 refund in April. Mathematically, you end up in the same place. But in real life? The person with $800 withheld is spending ten months with less money in their account than they need.

In 2020, the IRS overhauled the W-4. They ditched the old "allowances" system and replaced it with one that asks more specific questions about your income, deductions, and credits. The new form is more accurate if you fill it out correctly. But it's also more intimidating, which means a lot of people either skip the optional sections or just guess.

Don't guess.

What you need is fifteen minutes, your most recent tax return, and a willingness to actually engage with the form instead of just signing it and hoping for the best.

Let's walk through it.

Step 1: Personal Information

Name, address, Social Security number, filing status. The one thing to double-check is your filing status—single, married filing jointly, married filing separately, head of household. If you got married or divorced recently and you're still using your old status, fix it.

Step 2: Multiple Jobs or Spouse Works

If you or your spouse work more than one job at the same time, the IRS needs to know. Your employer only sees the income they pay you. If you work two jobs and each employer withholds based solely on what *they* pay, you're almost certainly going to underwithhold overall. Your combined income might push you into a higher tax bracket, but neither employer knows that.

The form gives you three options:

1. Use the IRS's online Tax Withholding Estimator. 2. Use the Multiple Jobs Worksheet in the W-4 instructions. 3. Check the box on Step 2(c) if there are only two jobs total and they pay roughly the same amount.

Option three is simplest, but it only works in very specific circumstances. For most people, the estimator is the way to go.

Step 3: Claim Dependents

If you have qualifying dependents—kids under seventeen, other relatives you support—you claim them here. This reduces your withholding because the IRS assumes you'll be claiming the Child Tax Credit or the Credit for Other Dependents when you file.

Here's the part people mess up: they either forget to claim dependents at all, which means they overwithhold, or they claim dependents they're not actually entitled to, which means they underwithhold and face penalties later. The rules for who qualifies are specific. Don't assume. Look it up.

And if you're divorced or separated and sharing custody, make sure you and your ex aren't *both* claiming the same kid. Only one of you gets the credit.

Step 4: Other Adjustments

This is the section most people skip. Don't.

There are three subsections:

- **(a) Other Income**: If you have income that's not subject to withholding—interest, dividends, retirement income, freelance earnings—you enter the estimated annual amount here. This increases your withholding to cover the tax on that other income.

- **(b) Deductions**: If you expect to claim deductions beyond the standard deduction—mortgage interest, charitable contributions, large medical expenses—you enter the estimated annual amount here. This *reduces* your withholding because the IRS assumes your taxable income will be lower.

- **(c) Extra Withholding**: If you want an additional specific dollar amount withheld from each paycheck, you enter it here.

Most people don't fill out subsections (a) and (b) because it requires thinking ahead. You have to estimate what your deductions and other income will be for the year. But if you *don't* do it, you're essentially telling the IRS, "Just guess." And their guess is going to be wrong.

Take Rachel. She and her husband itemize deductions every year—big mortgage, hefty property taxes, regular charitable giving. Their itemized deductions come to about $30,000, well above the standard deduction. But Rachel never filled out Step 4(b). So her employer withheld as if she were taking the standard deduction, which meant she overwithheld by a significant amount.

One year, she actually filled out the section. Her withholding dropped. Her paychecks went up by about $200 a month. That's $2,400 a year she had access to throughout the year instead of waiting until April.

Step 5: Sign and Date

Don't skip this. An unsigned W-4 isn't valid.

Now, about that IRS Tax Withholding Estimator.

It's free. It's online. And it's shockingly good, assuming you give it accurate information.

You'll need:

- Your most recent pay stub (or stubs, if you or your spouse have multiple jobs). - Your most recent tax return. - An estimate of any income not reported on a W-2. - An estimate of your deductions and credits for the year.

The estimator walks you through a series of questions, crunches the numbers, and tells you exactly what to put on your W-4. It even generates a printable summary you can hand to your employer's HR department.

Carlos used to just fill out his W-4 based on gut feel. Single, no dependents, one job—he figured it was straightforward. But he also maxed out his 401(k) contributions every year and made regular donations to his church, which meant his taxable income was lower than his gross income. For years, he got refunds of $1,500 or more.

Then he ran the estimator. Plugged in his salary, his 401(k) contributions, his charitable giving. The estimator told him he was overwithholding by about $130 a month. So he updated his W-4, and his paychecks went up. That extra $130 a month went straight into a high-yield savings account. By the end of the year, he had over $1,600 saved—more than he would've gotten as a refund, plus the interest it earned while sitting in his account instead of the government's.

It's not magic. It's just math. But you have to actually do the math.

Maria is a single mother with one kid. She works full-time making $60,000 a year. She rents, so no mortgage interest deduction. She takes the standard deduction.

For years, Maria claimed zero allowances on her old W-4, thinking that was the safest bet. Every April, she got a refund of around $1,200.

But then her car broke down in July. The repair was $900. She didn't have it. So she put it on a credit card and paid it off over six months, accumulating about $80 in interest. Meanwhile, $700 of "her" money was sitting with the IRS.

Using the estimator, Maria entered her income, claimed her daughter as a dependent, and indicated she takes the standard deduction. The estimator recommended she adjust her withholding so she'd break even at tax time. She updated her W-4. Her paychecks went up by about $100 a month. That $100 went into a savings account specifically for car repairs and other emergencies.

The next time something broke, she had the cash.

David and Sarah are married, filing jointly. David earns $80,000 at his day job. Sarah works part-time making $25,000 and also runs a small freelance graphic design business that brings in another $15,000 a year. They have two kids. They itemize deductions—mortgage interest, property taxes, charitable contributions—totaling about $20,000 annually.

They both just filled out their W-4s as "married filing jointly" and claimed their two kids. They didn't account for Sarah's freelance income at all. Every April, they owed between $800 and $1,200. Every April, it was a scramble.

Using the estimator, they entered both W-2 incomes, Sarah's estimated freelance income, their itemized deductions, and the Child Tax Credit for their two kids. The estimator recommended they check the "multiple jobs" box and add $75 per paycheck in extra withholding on David's W-4 to cover the taxes on Sarah's freelance income.

They updated their W-4s. The next April, they owed $140. Close enough. No scramble. No stress.

The goal is to get as close to zero as possible. You don't want a big refund. You don't want a big balance due. You want your withholding to match your actual tax liability so your money is working for you all year long.

If you're self-employed: the principles are exactly the same; the mechanics are just slightly different.

You don't fill out a W-4 because you don't have an employer withholding taxes. Instead, you're responsible for making estimated tax payments directly to the IRS four times a year using Form

1040-ES.

Let’s say you’re a freelance writer and you expect to make $70,000 this year. You have about $8,000 in business expenses. You contribute $5,000 to a SEP IRA. Your taxable income is $70,000 - $8,000 - $5,000 = $57,000.

Using the tax tables, you estimate your federal income tax liability at around $6,500. Divide that by four: $1,625 per quarter. You send that amount to the IRS in April, June, September, and January.

If you don’t make those quarterly payments and you owe more than $1,000 when you file, you can get hit with underpayment penalties.

And just like with the W-4, you need to revisit your estimated payments whenever your situation changes. If you land a big project and your income jumps, adjust your payments. If you have a slow quarter, you can reduce them.

Here’s a simple system for staying on top of this throughout the year.

The W-4 Checkup System:

1. **Set a recurring reminder for the first week of December.** Pull out your most recent tax return and compare it to your current pay stubs. Are you on track?

2. **Run the IRS Tax Withholding Estimator.** It takes ten minutes. Do it every December and whenever you have a major life

change—marriage, divorce, new baby, new job, significant raise.

3. **Update your W-4 based on the estimator's recommendations.** Don't second-guess it. Just follow what it says.

4. **Monitor your first paycheck after the update.** Make sure the withholding actually changed. Sometimes HR departments take a while to process updates, or they make errors.

5. **Check in again in March.** If you updated your W-4 in December, your first quarter should give you a sense of whether the new withholding is on track. If your refund or balance due is trending way off, adjust again.

That's it. Five steps. One recurring calendar reminder. And you'll never be caught off guard at tax time again.

The most common mistake people make with the W-4: filling it out once and never updating it.

Your W-4 isn't a static document. It's supposed to reflect your current situation. If you filled it out when you were single with no kids and you're now married with two kids, your withholding is almost certainly wrong.

Jennifer's daughter got her tubes in January, three months late, after the deductible reset—the scheduler was sympathetic but firm when she called back in December to reschedule. Fixing withholding solves the cash flow problem. But it doesn't solve the question of what you're withholding for.

The money's back in your paycheck now. The question is: where else has it been hiding?

Chapter 3: The Deduction Detective: Uncovering Hidden Savings

Warren Buffett once told a classroom full of business students that his tax rate was lower than his secretary's. This was 2007, Omaha, a Q&A; session that got maybe three paragraphs in the Wall Street Journal and then disappeared. Nobody made a fuss.

Most of us are the secretary in this story.

The standard deduction is clean. Simple. You claim it, you're done. No receipts, no calculations, no nagging feeling at 2 a.m. that you missed something. For most people, most years, it's the right move. I'm not here to tell you otherwise.

But here's the part nobody mentions when they tell you to "just take the standard deduction and save yourself the headache": the tax code isn't designed to minimize what you owe. It's designed to collect the maximum amount you'll tolerate without pushing back. Every deduction you see—every credit, every adjustment, every weird carve-out for some hyper-specific situation—exists because someone fought for it. Some industry lobby. Some coalition of accountants. Some group of people who convinced Congress that a particular kind of expense deserved special treatment.

And if you don't claim it? The IRS certainly won't send you a reminder.

This isn't adversarial, exactly. It's structural. The system assumes you know the rules and will advocate for yourself. If you don't, you lose by default. Not because anyone's out to get you—just because that's how the machine works.

I want to tell you something I've never put in writing before, mostly because it's embarrassing.

For three straight years—2014, 2015, 2016—I qualified for the home office deduction and never claimed it. Not because I didn't know it existed. I'd read Publication 587. I'd skimmed the worksheets. I'd even bookmarked the IRS page with the rules, thinking I'd get to it eventually. I just assumed it didn't apply to *me*.

The mental image I had of a "home office" was something out of a law firm: built-in bookshelves, mahogany desk, maybe one of those green-shaded banker's lamps. My setup was a folding table from Craigslist, a chair that squeaked when I leaned back, and a filing cabinet I'd found on the curb during someone else's move-out day. That's not a home office, I told myself. That's just a corner of my bedroom where I answer emails.

Turns out the IRS doesn't care whether your desk cost forty bucks or four thousand. They care whether the space is used regularly and exclusively for work. Mine was. I just never connected the dots.

I only caught the mistake when I was helping a friend file their return. She was a freelance writer, working from home, her setup nearly identical to mine—a desk, a chair, a cabinet, all used exclusively for work-related tasks. She claimed the home office deduction. I asked her how much it saved her. She pulled up her return: about $700 that year.

I went back and looked at my own returns. Three years. Roughly $2,100 left on the table because I'd convinced myself I didn't qualify.

That's the thing about deductions. They're not hiding. They're sitting there in plain sight, and most of us walk right past them because we've decided they're for someone else—someone more organized, someone with fancier circumstances, someone who "really needs it." But the IRS doesn't operate on need. It operates on eligibility. Either you meet the requirements or you don't, and if you do, the money is yours to keep.

So let's talk about what you're actually entitled to claim. And more importantly, whether it's worth your time.

Most tax conversations start in exactly the wrong place. They hit you with rules, thresholds, IRS publication numbers, and your brain shuts down before you even get to the part that matters. I'm going to give you the framework first—the skeleton you can hang everything else on—and then we'll fill in the details.

You have two options when you file: the standard deduction or itemized deductions. Not both. Pick one.

The standard deduction is a flat amount the IRS lets you subtract from your income just for existing as a taxpayer. For 2023, that was $13,850 if you filed as single, $27,700 if you filed jointly as a married couple. These numbers adjust for inflation each year, so don't assume last year's figures still apply—using outdated numbers is a quick way to mess up your math and either leave money on the table or trigger an audit.

Itemizing means you list out specific, qualified expenses—medical bills over a certain threshold, mortgage interest, state and local taxes, charitable donations—and if the total exceeds the standard deduction, you come out ahead. If it doesn't, you've just created extra paperwork for yourself and gained nothing.

The question most people never ask is: *When does itemizing actually make sense?*

And the answer is simpler than the tax prep industry wants you to believe. You itemize when the math says you should. That's it. Not when it feels right, not when your neighbor swears by it, not when some random finance blog tells you it's "the smart move for high earners." When your qualified deductions add up to more than the standard deduction for your filing status, you itemize. When they don't, you take the standard deduction and move on.

Let me show you what this looks like when it's not theoretical.

Sarah is a single mom outside Phoenix. Three-bedroom house, still paying the mortgage. In 2023, she paid $8,000 in mortgage interest. That's money already gone—vanished into the bank every month—and it hurts a little every time she thinks about it. She's also dealing with lingering issues from a car accident two years back, which means physical therapy twice a week, sometimes three times if her shoulder flares up. After insurance, she paid $4,500 out of pocket for medical expenses. And because she believes in putting her money where her values are, she donated $6,000 throughout the year—mostly to a local food bank and an organization that provides school supplies to kids whose families can't afford them.

Add it up: $8,000 + $4,500 + $6,000 = $18,500.

That sounds like a lot. It *is* a lot. Sarah's sitting there at her kitchen table in March, calculator in hand, thinking, *Okay, $18,500 is definitely more than the $13,850 standard deduction, so I should itemize.*

Wrong.

And this is where the tax code stops being straightforward and starts being the tax code.

Medical expenses? You can only deduct the amount that exceeds 7.5% of your adjusted gross income. Sarah’s AGI is $65,000. Seven and a half percent of that is $4,875. Her out-of-pocket medical costs were $4,500—which is *less* than the threshold, even after months of physical therapy and a couple of specialist visits she had to pay for upfront because her insurance wouldn’t pre-approve them.

So she gets zero. Not a dollar. Not even the difference.

That drops her itemized total from $18,500 to $14,000—mortgage interest plus charitable donations. Still more than the standard deduction, but barely. And here’s the thing nobody tells you: itemizing means more paperwork, more documentation, more potential for the IRS to send you a letter six months later asking you to prove that donation you made in February. For an extra $150 in deductions—which translates to maybe $30 or $40 in actual tax savings, depending on her bracket—is it worth it?

Sarah takes the standard deduction. She spends her Saturday at her daughter’s soccer game instead of sorting receipts. She made the right call.

Now let’s flip it.

Mark and Lisa are married with two kids, homeowners in a state with high property taxes. 2023 was an expensive year. They paid $12,000 in mortgage interest, $7,000 out of pocket for medical expenses—Lisa had surgery, and even with decent insurance, the bills piled up—and donated $8,000 to their church and a few other causes they care about. They also paid $5,000 in state and local taxes.

Quick math: $12,000 + $7,000 + $8,000 + $5,000 = $32,000.

The standard deduction for married couples filing jointly in 2023 was $27,700. So Mark and Lisa are looking at this and thinking, *Okay, we're itemizing. This is obvious.*

Maybe. Let's walk through it, because nothing is ever as obvious as it looks.

First, the medical expense threshold. Their combined AGI is $95,000. Seven and a half percent of that is $7,125. Their medical expenses were $7,000—just under the threshold. Zero deduction. Again.

You'd think that after spending $7,000 on medical bills in a single year—surgery, recovery, follow-up appointments, the whole nightmare—you'd at least get to deduct *something*. But the tax code doesn't care what you think is fair. It cares what crosses the threshold. Mark and Lisa don't. They're out.

Second, the state and local tax (SALT) deduction has a cap: $10,000 per household, no matter how much you actually paid. Mark and Lisa only paid $5,000, so they're fine on that front. But if they lived in New York or California and had paid $15,000 or $20,000—which isn't remotely unusual in high-tax states—they'd still be capped at $10,000. The rest? Gone. Not deductible.

So their actual itemized deductions are: $12,000 (mortgage interest) + $8,000 (charitable donations) + $5,000 (SALT) = $25,000.

That's $2,700 *less* than the standard deduction.

Mark and Lisa take the standard deduction. They don't itemize. And they feel vaguely cheated, because they did everything right—paid their mortgage, donated to charity, dealt with a medical crisis—and the system still told them to take the easier path because the math didn't work out.

You see the trap? It's not enough to know what categories exist. You have to know the rules within each category—the thresholds, the caps, the fine print that turns a big number into nothing at all. This is where most people give up. They assume it's too complicated, too much work, too easy to screw up. So they take the standard deduction every year and never think about it again.

But here's what I need you to understand: the complexity isn't there to scare you off. It's there because the tax code is trying to balance fairness—or at least the appearance of fairness—across millions of different financial situations. And yes, that means rules and thresholds and caps. But it also means opportunities, if you know where to look.

I'm going to walk you through a process I call the Deduction Threshold Check. It's not fancy. It's designed to answer one question: *Is itemizing worth my time this year?*

Step 1: Estimate your itemized deductions.

Go through your records—bank statements, credit card bills, donation receipts, mortgage statements—and total up your potential deductions in each major category. Medical expenses, mortgage interest, state and local taxes, charitable donations. Be realistic. Only include amounts you *know* qualify based on the actual IRS rules, not what you hope might qualify if you squint at the guidelines hard enough.

Step 2: Compare to the standard deduction.

Look up the standard deduction for your filing status for the tax year you're filing. It's on the IRS website. Takes thirty seconds.

Step 3: Run the check.

If your estimated itemized deductions are meaningfully greater than the standard deduction—and I mean by at least a few hundred dollars, not $20—itemizing probably makes sense. If they're less, or even close, stick with the standard deduction. The time and stress you'll save is worth more than squeezing out an extra $50 in tax savings.

Let's run this on a real scenario.

Carlos is twenty-eight, single, renting an apartment in Austin. He's been paying off student loans for six years now, and last year he paid $4,000 in interest. That's $4,000 that didn't go toward the principal, didn't reduce what he owes—just disappeared into the loan servicer's pocket. He also had some unexpected dental work—a root canal and a crown—that cost him $6,000 out of pocket after his insurance covered what it was willing to cover, which wasn't much. And because he cares about certain causes, he donated $3,000 throughout the year, mostly through monthly contributions to a couple of environmental nonprofits.

His potential itemized deductions: $6,000 (medical) + $4,000 (student loan interest) + $3,000 (charitable) = $13,000.

The standard deduction for single filers in 2023 was $13,850. So Carlos is right on the edge. Maybe he figures it's worth itemizing just to see if he can squeeze out a little extra, right?

Not quite.

Carlos's AGI is $72,000. The medical expense threshold is 7.5% of that, which comes out to $5,400. His out-of-pocket medical costs were $6,000. So he can deduct the amount over the threshold: $600. Not $6,000. Six hundred dollars.

And here's the kicker, the thing that trips people up every single year: student loan interest isn't an itemized deduction. It's what's called an *above-the-line* deduction, which means Carlos can claim it *regardless* of whether he itemizes or takes the standard deduction. So it doesn't factor into this comparison at all. It's separate. He gets to claim it either way.

His actual itemized total: $600 (medical) + $3,000 (charitable) = $3,600.

The standard deduction is $13,850. If Carlos itemized, he'd be leaving over $10,000 on the table. He takes the standard deduction, claims his $4,000 student loan interest deduction separately, and he's done.

Now, you might be thinking: *This sounds like a lot of effort just to figure out I should do the simple thing.*

And you're right. It is. But here's why it matters.

If you never run the check, you'll never know if you're one of the people who *should* be itemizing. You'll never catch the year where your medical expenses spike because of an unexpected surgery, or you buy a house and suddenly have mortgage interest to claim, or you decide to make a large charitable donation after selling some stock and you want to offset the capital gains. Those are the years where itemizing saves you real money—hundreds, sometimes thousands of dollars. But if you're not paying attention, if you're just defaulting to the standard deduction because it's easier, you'll miss it.

The tax code doesn't reward passivity. It rewards attention.

So what should you actually be tracking throughout the year? Not at tax time, when it's too late to do anything about it, but *now*, while you still have time to find receipts and document what you spent.

Start with medical expenses, even if they feel small.

I know what you're thinking—if you didn't hit the 7.5% threshold this year, what's the point? Here's the point: you might hit it next year. Or the year after. And if you haven't been keeping records, you'll have no idea what you actually spent. You'll end up guessing, or worse, leaving it off entirely because you can't prove it.

Doctor visits, prescriptions, hospital stays, dental work, vision care, even mileage to and from medical appointments—all of it counts, as long as it wasn't reimbursed by insurance. The IRS sets a standard rate each year for medical mileage. In 2023, it was 22 cents per mile for the first half of the year, then bumped up to 22 cents for the second half. (These rates change, so always check the current year's rate before you calculate.)

Keep the receipts. All of them. Even the $15 co-pay that feels too small to bother with. You'd be surprised how quickly those add up over twelve months.

Next: student loan interest.

This one's straightforward, and honestly, it's one of the few parts of the tax code that actually works in your favor without a lot of hoops to jump through. If you paid interest on a qualified student loan, you can deduct up to $2,500 per year, and you don't have to itemize to claim it. Your loan servicer will send you a Form 1098-E at the end of the year showing exactly how much you paid.

But—and this is important—double-check it. Servicers make mistakes. If you refinanced mid-year, or if you switched servicers, the form might not show the full amount you actually paid. Pull up your own records and compare. If there's a discrepancy, you can claim the correct amount on your return; just keep documentation in case the IRS asks.

If you're an educator—kindergarten through twelfth grade, public or private—there's a small but meaningful deduction for unreimbursed classroom expenses. Up to $300 of your own money spent on books, supplies, software, equipment, or other materials for your students. It's not itemized. You claim it on top of the standard deduction.

I know $300 doesn't sound like much when you're spending that every month out of your own pocket because your school's budget is a joke and the district won't reimburse you for basic supplies. But it's $300 the IRS is offering you, and you might as well take it. It's there. It's yours. Claim it.

Then there's charitable donations.

Cash contributions to qualified 501(c)(3) organizations are the easy ones—you write a check, you get a receipt (or you should), you deduct the amount. But non-cash donations count too, and this is where people leave money on the table without realizing it.

That bag of clothes you dropped off at Goodwill last spring? Deductible. The old furniture you donated to Habitat for Humanity when you moved? Deductible. Even a car, if you donate it to a qualified organization and they actually use it for their mission instead of just selling it for scrap.

Here's the catch: for non-cash donations over $500, you need documentation. Either a detailed receipt from the charity showing what you donated and its fair market value, or an appraisal if the items are worth more than $5,000.

And "fair market value" doesn't mean what you paid for it ten years ago. It means what someone would reasonably pay for it *now*, in its current condition. That five-year-old coat you donated? Maybe worth $10 or $15, not the $150 you spent on it at Nordstrom back when you thought you'd wear it more than twice.

The IRS publishes guidelines for valuing donated goods, and they're strict. If you claim $5,000 for a carload of old clothes and kitchen stuff, you're going to get questions. Be realistic. Be honest. The deduction is worth taking, but not if it triggers an audit that costs you more in time and stress than you saved.

Let me show you what this actually looks like in practice. Not in theory, not in some sanitized example from a textbook, but sitting at your kitchen table in mid-March with a pile of mail you haven't opened and a growing sense of dread.

It's three weeks until the filing deadline. You've been meaning to get organized all year—you really have—but life got in the way. It always does. And now you're staring at a shoebox full of receipts, a stack of unopened envelopes, and the creeping realization that if you don't figure this out soon, you're filing an extension and dealing with it in October.

First step: pull out your mortgage statement.

If you own a home, your lender is required to send you a Form 1098 showing how much interest you paid during the year. It's usually in the mail by early February, sometimes late January. That number—whatever it is—goes straight into your itemized deduction calculation. No math required, no guesswork. Just copy the number from Box 1 of the form.

Next: medical expenses. This is where the shoebox comes in.

Go through every receipt, every explanation of benefits (EOB) from your insurance company, every billing statement from doctors and hospitals and pharmacies. Total up what you paid out of pocket—not what the provider charged, not what insurance theoretically covered, but what actually came out of *your* checking account or went on *your* credit card.

Include prescriptions. Co-pays. Dental work. Vision care. Medical equipment—crutches, braces, blood pressure monitors, whatever you had to buy because of a medical condition. Even over-the-counter items if they were prescribed by a doctor. (The IRS is surprisingly specific about this: you can't deduct Tylenol you bought at CVS on your own, but you can deduct it if your doctor wrote you a prescription for it and you have documentation.)

Now calculate 7.5% of your AGI. Your AGI is on line 11 of last year's Form 1040, or you can estimate it based on this year's income if it hasn't changed much. Multiply by 0.075. Subtract that number from your total medical expenses.

If the result is positive, that's your deductible amount. If it's zero or negative, you don't get a medical deduction this year. It's frustrating, especially if you spent thousands of dollars on medical care, but that's the rule.

Move on to charitable donations.

Gather your receipts—cash donations, acknowledgment letters from charities, bank statements showing recurring monthly contributions. Add them up. That's your charitable deduction. Simple. (Well, mostly simple. If you donated more than $250 to any single organization, you need a written acknowledgment from that organization to claim it. If you didn't get one, email them now and ask. Most nonprofits will send it without any hassle.)

Finally: state and local taxes.

If you paid state income tax throughout the year, it'll show up on your W-2 in Box 17, or you can check your final paystub from December. If you paid property tax on your home, it'll be on your mortgage statement (if your lender collects it through escrow) or on the bill you get directly from your county tax assessor.

Add them together. But remember: the total is capped at $10,000. If you paid $8,000, you can deduct $8,000. If you paid $15,000, you can only deduct $10,000. The rest vanishes.

Now add up all your itemized deductions: mortgage interest + medical expenses (if any) + charitable donations + SALT (up to $10,000).

Compare that total to the standard deduction for your filing status.

If your itemized total is higher—meaningfully higher, not just by $50 or $100—congratulations, you're itemizing this year. Gather your documentation, fill out Schedule A, attach it to your Form 1040. If it's not higher, you're taking the standard deduction, and that's fine. Either way, you've done the math. You know you're not leaving money on the table.

But here's the part most people skip. The part that actually matters if you want to stop scrambling every March like this.

You need a system. Not next year. Not eventually. Now.

You don't need fancy software. You don't need a degree in accounting. You don't even need to be particularly organized, as long as you're willing to spend five seconds every time a potentially deductible expense happens.

Here's what you do: create a folder. Physical or digital, doesn't matter. Label it "Tax Deductions [Year]."

Every time you incur an expense that might be deductible—medical bill, charitable donation, mortgage statement at the end of the year, receipt for work supplies if you're an educator—put it in the folder. That's it. Five seconds.

If you want to get slightly more organized, create subfolders by category: Medical, Charitable, Home, Education, Work. When a receipt comes in, file it immediately under the right category. Then, when tax season arrives, you're not sifting through a pile of random paper trying to figure out what that $47 charge from last April was for. You already know.

I know this sounds absurdly basic. It is. But the reason most people don't claim deductions they're entitled to isn't because the rules are too complicated—it's because they don't have the documentation when they need it. They paid for something six months ago, tossed the receipt, and now they can't prove it happened. So they don't claim it. They leave money on the table, not because they want to, but because the tax code doesn't care what you *think* you spent. It cares what you can *prove* you spent.

And proof requires records.

Let me tell you about Angela. She's a friend of mine, freelance graphic designer, which means her income swings wildly from month to month and her expenses are even less predictable. For years, she handled her taxes the way most freelancers do: by panicking in early April and hoping for the best.

Then one year—2019, I think—she hired an accountant to clean up the mess. The accountant asked for her business expense records. Software subscriptions, stock photo licenses, mileage for client meetings, home office costs. Angela handed over what she had, which wasn't much. A few crumpled receipts. Some credit card statements with charges circled in pen. A lot of shrugging and saying, "I think I bought that in March? Maybe February?"

The accountant did the best she could. But Angela walked away knowing she'd missed deductions. Probably hundreds of dollars' worth. Maybe more. She just didn't have the documentation to claim them.

So she built a system.

Nothing fancy. Just a folder on her computer labeled "Taxes," with subfolders for each category of expense: Software, Travel,

Office, Equipment. Whenever she bought something for the business—Adobe subscription, new external hard drive, gas for a trip to meet a client—she'd scan the receipt or take a photo with her phone and save it in the appropriate subfolder. Once a month, she'd spend maybe fifteen minutes updating a simple spreadsheet: date, description, amount, category.

That's it. Fifteen minutes a month. Sometimes less if it was a slow month.

The next year, when she sat down with her accountant, she had everything ready. Every expense documented, categorized, totaled. The accountant didn't have to chase her down for missing receipts or make judgment calls about whether something counted as a business expense. It was all there.

Angela's tax bill dropped by over $3,000 compared to the year before. Not because her income changed—it actually went up slightly—but because she was finally claiming everything she was entitled to. Home office deduction, business use of her car, equipment depreciation, professional development courses. All of it documented, all of it legitimate, all of it money she got to keep instead of handing over to the IRS.

She didn't become a tax expert. She didn't spend hours studying IRS publications or watching YouTube videos about Schedule C. She just built a system—a stupid simple system, really—and stuck with it.

You can do the same thing. You probably should. Because here's the truth nobody wants to say out loud: the difference between people who pay too much in taxes and people who don't isn't intelligence, or income level, or access to expensive accountants. It's attention. It's knowing what to track and actually tracking it. It's being willing to spend fifteen minutes a month building a record instead of scrambling for three days every April trying to reconstruct the past year from memory and credit card statements.

The tax code is what it is. You can complain about it—and believe me, I get it, the complaints are valid—but complaining doesn't change your tax bill. Documentation does. Systems do. Paying attention does.

So start now. Today, if you can. Create the folder. Set a monthly reminder to update your records. It won't feel important at first. It'll feel like busywork, like something you could skip this month because you don't have that many expenses anyway and you'll definitely remember to do it next month.

Don't skip it. Because the whole point of a system isn't that it works when you feel motivated or when the stakes are high. The point is that it works when you're tired, when you're busy, when you'd rather be doing literally anything else. The system runs even when you don't feel like running it, and six months from now—or a year, or three years—you'll be sitting at your kitchen table in March, and instead of panicking, you'll just open the folder and get to work.

And that medical bill you're looking at right now, the one that just came in the mail? The one you're about to toss in a drawer and forget about?

Put it in the folder.

Because here's what happens when you don't: you lose the receipt. Or you remember the receipt but you can't remember what it was for. Or you remember what it was for but you can't prove it was necessary. Or you can prove it was necessary but you've thrown out the documentation that would have made it deductible. And then April comes, and you're sitting there with your tax software open, staring at a blank field that says "medical expenses," and you have this vague memory of spending a lot on healthcare this year, but you can't remember how much or when or whether any of it actually counts.

So you skip it. You leave it blank. You take the standard deduction instead of itemizing because itemizing requires proof and you don't have proof because you didn't put it in the folder.

And you've just left money on the table. Not hypothetical money. Not "maybe if the market does well" money. Actual money that you spent, that you could have written off, that would have reduced your taxable income and put cash back in your pocket.

Let's be specific about what you're actually looking for, because "medical expenses" sounds simple until you start digging and realize it's not.

You're not just tracking doctor visits. You're tracking mileage to and from medical appointments—because yes, that's deductible if you're itemizing. You're tracking co-pays and prescription costs, obviously, but you're also tracking over-the-counter medications that were prescribed by your doctor, because those count too. You're tracking dental work. Vision care. Hearing aids. Medical equipment. Home modifications if they're medically necessary. You're tracking insurance premiums that you paid out of pocket, not the ones your employer paid.

You're tracking things that don't feel like medical expenses but absolutely are. The special mattress your doctor told you to buy for your back. The air purifier for your asthma. The service dog. The weight-loss program if it was prescribed to treat a specific diagnosed condition, not just because you felt like losing weight.

This is why people give up. Because it's not one thing. It's forty things. And nobody tells you which forty things until you're already past the deadline and it's too late.

But if you've been putting it in the folder all year, you don't have to remember. The folder remembers. The folder doesn't care whether it felt like a medical expense at the time. It just knows you spent three hundred dollars on physical therapy in June and here's the receipt.

Now expand this out. Because medical expenses are just one category.

Business expenses if you're self-employed or freelancing. Charitable donations—and not just the cash you dropped in the bucket at church, but the mileage you drove to volunteer at the food bank, the supplies you bought for the school fundraiser, the old clothes you donated to Goodwill if you got a receipt and documented the value. Education expenses if you're taking classes that maintain or improve skills in your current job. Job search expenses if you're looking for work in your current field. Home office expenses if you're working from home and meet the IRS requirements, which are stricter than most people think but not impossible.

Energy-efficient home improvements. State and local taxes. Mortgage interest. Property taxes. Investment expenses. Casualty and theft losses if they meet the threshold.

Every single one of these has rules. Every single one has documentation requirements. Every single one has people who qualify and don't know it, and people who think they qualify and don't.

And you're not going to figure out which category you're in by Googling it on April 10th. You're going to figure it out by tracking it all year, by keeping everything, and then either learning the rules yourself or handing the folder to someone who already knows them.

Here's the part nobody mentions: tracking expenses doesn't just save you money at tax time. It changes how you see money.

Because once you start writing things down, you start noticing patterns. You start seeing where your money actually goes, not where you think it goes. You start realizing that you've been spending sixty dollars a month on a subscription you forgot you had. You start realizing that your "occasional" takeout habit is actually four hundred dollars a month. You start realizing that the thing you thought was a one-time expense keeps happening every quarter like clockwork.

And now you have options. Not because someone lectured you about budgeting. Not because you're trying to be virtuous. But because you have information, and information is what lets you make actual decisions instead of just reacting to whatever your bank balance happens to be when you check it.

This is the part that feels boring until it isn't. Until you're sitting across from a financial advisor or a tax professional or a loan officer, and they ask you a question about your finances, and instead of shrugging and guessing, you pull out your folder and tell them exactly what they need to know.

Until you're negotiating a medical bill and you can pull up every payment you've made this year and show them, line by line, that you've already paid more than they're claiming.

Until you're applying for a mortgage and they want to see proof of income and expenses, and you have it. Not because you knew six months ago that you'd need it, but because you kept it anyway.

The system isn't sexy. It doesn't promise to make you rich. It doesn't have a motivational tagline or a twelve-step framework or a celebrity endorsement. It's just a folder and a habit and a commitment to writing things down.

But it's the difference between feeling like money is happening to you and knowing that you're the one making the decisions. It's the difference between hoping you didn't miss anything and knowing you didn't. It's the difference between tax season being something you dread and tax season being something you handle.

So here's your homework, and it's not complicated.

Get a folder. Label it. Put the medical bill in it. Put the receipt from the pharmacy in it. Put the mileage log in it. Put everything in it that even remotely looks like it might matter later, because later you can always throw it out, but you can't go back in time and un-lose it.

Do this every week. Not when you feel like it. Not when you remember. Every week, same day, same time. Make it automatic. Make it boring. Make it the kind of thing you do without thinking, like brushing your teeth or locking the front door.

And then, when April comes, you'll open the folder and everything you need will be there.

Not because you're incredibly organized. Not because you love paperwork. But because you built a system, and the system worked.

His secretary filed her return, took the standard deduction, moved on with her life. Buffett? He understood what was available and claimed it.

Buffett's secretary claimed the standard deduction and moved on. Buffett claimed everything that was his. But there's one category where the government doesn't just let you claim money—they'll match you dollar for dollar, and millions of people still say no.

Chapter 4: Retirement Contributions as Tax Shields

When was the last time someone offered to match you, dollar for dollar, on money you were already planning to save? And when was the last time you said no?

The number was something absurd. Billions with a B. I don't remember the exact figure and I'm not going to make one up, but it was big enough that I sat there with my oil change taking twenty minutes longer than they'd promised, doing napkin math on the back of my receipt, trying to figure out if I was one of the people they were talking about.

I was.

I'd set my contribution to three percent when I got hired, because three felt like a reasonable number—more than zero, less than a lot—and then I'd never looked at it again. Turns out my employer matched dollar-for-dollar up to six percent, which meant they were offering to literally double everything I put in, up to that cap, and I was leaving half of it unclaimed because I hadn't bothered to read the benefits packet they'd handed me on my first day. Nobody followed up. Nobody from HR called to say, "Hey, you know you're walking past free money, right?" Why would they? It wasn't their money. It was mine, and I just… wasn't taking it.

Three years of that. Three years at a salary of about fifty-four thousand, which meant I'd missed out on roughly eight hundred dollars per year in matching contributions. Twenty-four hundred total. Plus whatever that twenty-four hundred would've grown into if it had actually been sitting in the market instead of staying in the company's pocket.

I changed it that afternoon. Logged into the benefits portal from my phone in the Jiffy Lube parking lot, bumped my contribution to six percent, watched my projected annual match number update in real time. It felt like finding money in a coat pocket, except the coat was one I'd been wearing every day and somehow never checked.

The thing that stuck with me wasn't the twenty-four hundred, though. It was the realization that the system is designed to let you fail passively. You don't have to make a bad decision. You just have to make no decision, or make one decision once and never revisit it, and the IRS will happily collect the maximum you'll tolerate without pushing back. The retirement account structure isn't there because the government loves you and wants you to prosper. It's there because if you don't save for your own retirement, you'll end up depending on a Social Security system that's already running on fumes, or on means-tested programs that cost the Treasury even more than just giving you a tax break up front.

So they've built in incentives. Put money in a retirement account, and we won't tax it this year. Or, depending on the type, we won't tax it ever—not the contributions, not the gains, nothing. You can take that deal or leave it. But leaving it doesn't make you disciplined or skeptical of the system. It just makes you poorer.

Here's what most people don't grasp, and I didn't either for the longest time: retirement contributions aren't about self-denial or deferring gratification. That's the framing, sure, because it makes the whole thing sound virtuous and responsible, but it's not what's actually happening. What's happening is you're putting up a barrier between your income and the IRS before they get a chance to tax it. You're not sacrificing. You're defending.

Think of it like this. Every dollar you earn walks through a corridor. At the end of that corridor, there's a booth, and the IRS is sitting there with their hand out. Twenty-two cents, thirty-two cents, whatever your marginal rate is. You can let every dollar walk straight through and pay the toll. Or you can pull some of those dollars aside *before* they get to the booth, route them through a different door marked "retirement account," and the IRS just… watches them go. They'll get their cut eventually, maybe, depending on the account type. But not today. And in the meantime, that money compounds without getting skimmed.

The simplest version of this—and I'm going to walk through the mechanics because I've found that most people's understanding of retirement accounts is vague enough that they can't actually articulate how the tax benefit works—is the traditional IRA.

Individual Retirement Account. You open one at any brokerage—Vanguard, Fidelity, Schwab, whoever. They're all fine. You contribute money to it, and that money is earmarked for retirement, meaning you're not supposed to touch it until fifty-nine and a half unless you want to pay penalties. The "traditional" part means you contribute pre-tax dollars. Your contribution reduces your taxable income for the year.

Example: you earn sixty thousand, you contribute six thousand to a traditional IRA, the IRS treats you as if you only earned fifty-four. You pay taxes on fifty-four, not sixty.

This is not an arcane loophole. It's written into the tax code on purpose. Congress wants you to save because the alternative—millions of people hitting retirement age with nothing saved, all leaning on a Social Security system that was never designed to be anyone's sole income source—is a fiscal disaster nobody wants to deal with.

Contribution limits change every year. They adjust for inflation. As I'm writing this it's sixty-five hundred if you're under fifty, seventy-five hundred if you're fifty or older. By the time you're reading this it might be higher. Don't trust a number from a book. Look it up on the IRS website.

Let's say you're in the twenty-two percent federal tax bracket. Not uncommon if you're single and making somewhere between forty-five and ninety-five thousand, depending on the year and what deductions you're taking. You max out a traditional IRA at sixty-five hundred. That sixty-five hundred would have been taxed at twenty-two percent—fourteen hundred thirty dollars straight to the Treasury. Instead, you contributed it, so your taxable income drops by sixty-five hundred, and your tax bill drops by fourteen hundred thirty.

You still have the sixty-five hundred. It's just sitting in an account at Fidelity instead of your checking account. And you've kept fourteen hundred thirty that otherwise would have evaporated.

Now—and I can hear the objection forming because I've had this conversation enough times to predict it word-for-word—you're thinking, "Sure, but I'll pay taxes on it eventually when I take it out in retirement, so I'm not really saving anything, I'm just delaying the inevitable."

Okay. Yes. Technically true. But delay is valuable, and here's why.

First, you might be in a lower tax bracket when you retire. You're in the twenty-two percent bracket now because you're pulling a salary. At sixty-five, you're not working anymore. You're living off Social Security, maybe a pension if you're extremely lucky, and whatever you've saved. Your effective tax rate could easily be twelve percent, or even lower if you're strategic about withdrawal timing. That means you avoided a twenty-two percent hit now and only paid twelve percent later. You arbitraged the difference. That's a real, no-asterisks win.

Second—and this is the piece that doesn't get enough attention—the money grows tax-deferred in the meantime. You invest that sixty-five hundred and it doubles over fifteen years. Now you've got thirteen thousand in the account. Yes, you'll owe tax on the full thirteen when you withdraw. But if you'd invested in a regular taxable brokerage account, you would have been paying taxes *along the way*. Capital gains every time you rebalanced. Dividends every year they got distributed. That drag compounds. The tax-deferred account grows faster because nothing's getting skimmed off the top every April.

I knew someone—let's call her Sarah, though that's not her real name and I'm not going to pretend I remember her exact salary down to the dollar—who started maxing out a traditional IRA at age thirty. She was earning something in the low sixties at the time, solidly in the twenty-two percent bracket. Every year, she put in the max. Every year, her tax bill dropped by about fourteen hundred bucks just from the deduction.

She kept this up for thirty-five years. Didn't miss a contribution. Didn't try to time the market or get cute with asset allocation. Just: max contribution, every year, invested in a boring mix of stock index funds.

At a seven percent average annual return—which is conservative for a diversified stock portfolio over that kind of horizon; the S&P; 500 has historically done closer to ten, even accounting for crashes and corrections—her account balance at sixty-five was north of nine hundred thousand dollars.

If Sarah had invested the same money in a taxable account instead, paying taxes on dividends and capital gains every year, she'd have ended up with significantly less. How much less depends on specifics I don't have—her exact tax rates, the turnover in her portfolio, whether she was doing any tax-loss harvesting—but we're talking a difference in the several hundred thousand dollar range. Maybe more.

And before you say it: yes, I know seven percent isn't guaranteed. Nothing's guaranteed. Markets crash. Recessions happen. If you want to stress-test the numbers at five percent to account for a particularly brutal sequence of returns, go ahead. It's still a compelling case. The point isn't that you'll definitely end up with nine hundred thousand. The point is that tax-deferred compounding, over multiple decades, turns a modest annual contribution into a sum that's genuinely life-changing, and ignoring that because you're worried about volatility means you don't understand how long-term investing actually works.

But maybe that's not your situation. Maybe you're young, early in your career, making decent money now but reasonably expecting to make a lot more in twenty years. If that's the case, paying taxes now at a low rate and never paying them again might be smarter than deferring taxes until you're in a higher bracket later.

That's where the Roth IRA comes in.

Roth IRAs flip the whole structure. You contribute after-tax dollars—money the IRS has already taken their cut of—so there's no deduction this year. But every dollar of growth, every cent of capital gains, every dividend, every dollar you pull out in retirement, is completely tax-free. Not tax-deferred. Tax-*free*.

If you're twenty-five, in the twelve percent bracket now, but you're reasonably confident you'll be in the twenty-four or thirty-two percent bracket in retirement because your career trajectory is strong and you're expecting significant income growth, paying twelve percent now and locking in zero percent forever is one of the best deals in the entire tax code.

You contribute seven thousand—current limit for someone under fifty, though again, check the IRS site because these numbers adjust—and you let it sit for forty years. Forty years of compounding does things to money that feel almost magical if you're not used to seeing it. Let's say it grows to one-point-four million. Aggressive? Maybe. But not implausible if you're starting young and the market cooperates.

When you pull that money out, you don't owe a dime. Not on the contributions. Not on the gains. Nothing.

Compare that to a traditional IRA, where you'd owe ordinary income tax on the full one-point-four million as you drew it down. If you're in the twenty-four percent bracket at that point, you're handing the IRS roughly three hundred thirty-six thousand dollars over the course of your retirement. The Roth costs you zero.

The catch—because there's always a catch, and the tax code never gives you something for nothing without some kind of strings attached—is that Roths have income limits. Make too much and you can't contribute directly. As of right now, single filers start getting phased out around one hundred forty thousand in modified adjusted gross income, completely cut off somewhere north of one-sixty. Married filing jointly, phaseout starts around two-twenty, complete shutoff around two-forty. These numbers inch up every year for inflation, so by the time you're reading this they'll probably be higher.

There's a workaround called the backdoor Roth—contribute to a traditional IRA, then immediately convert it to a Roth—but it gets complicated fast if you already have pre-tax traditional IRA balances sitting around, because of something called the pro-rata rule, which forces you to calculate conversions across all your IRA accounts and will absolutely screw you if you're not careful. I'm not getting into that here. This book is about moves you can execute on your own without needing to hire someone.

So the question becomes: traditional or Roth?

The answer depends entirely on whether you think your tax rate now is higher or lower than it'll be in retirement. Lower now? Roth makes sense. Higher now? Traditional. The problem, of course, is that nobody actually knows what their tax bracket will be in thirty years. You don't know what Congress will do. You don't know how much you'll be earning, or spending, or what the Social Security benefit will look like, or if the whole system will have imploded by then and we'll all be bartering with chickens.

You can make an educated guess, though, and an educated guess is enough. You don't need perfect information to make a good decision. Early in your career, low income, reasonable expectation of salary growth? Roth is probably the smarter bet. Peak earning years, high bracket, planning to downshift in retirement? Traditional makes more sense.

Here's one way I've seen people think through it without getting paralyzed: pull up last year's tax return. Look at your effective tax rate. Not your marginal rate—the rate on your last dollar of income—but your effective rate. Total tax divided by total income.

Let's say it's fifteen percent. Now picture yourself at sixty-five. You're not working. You're living off Social Security, maybe some part-time consulting income, and whatever you've saved. What do you think your effective rate will be then? Ten percent, because you're pulling less income overall? If you think it'll be lower, lean traditional. If you think it'll be higher—maybe because you're expecting rental income, or an inheritance, or you just think tax rates in general are going up because the national debt is spiraling and somebody's going to have to pay for it eventually—Roth is the safer play.

Or—and this is what I did for a while when I genuinely couldn't figure out which way to bet—you split the difference. Contribute to both. There's no rule that says you have to pick one. Total contributions still can't exceed the annual cap, but within that limit you can divide it however you want. Half in a traditional, half in a Roth. Or sixty-forty, or whatever ratio feels right to you.

That gives you tax diversification. Some money you'll pay taxes on later, some you've already paid taxes on. When you retire, you can pull from whichever account makes the most sense based on your tax situation that year. It's hedging, and honestly, it let me sleep better. I did this for about five years before I shifted entirely to Roth once my income trajectory became clearer. But splitting contributions when you're uncertain is a perfectly reasonable move. Better than doing nothing because you can't decide which one is optimal.

Now let's talk about the workplace accounts, because this is where most people actually build the bulk of their retirement savings, and also where the most free money gets left on the table.

If your employer offers a 401(k)—or a 403(b) if you work for a nonprofit or in government, same basic mechanics—you can contribute pre-tax dollars just like a traditional IRA. The money comes out of your paycheck before taxes get calculated, which drops your taxable income for the year. Same shield, just bigger limits.

Current caps are somewhere around twenty-three thousand per year if you're under fifty, closer to thirty if you're over. That's a hell of a lot more room than an IRA gives you. But the real story with 401(k)s isn't the contribution limit. It's the match.

A lot of employers—not all, but a lot—will match some portion of what you put in. They'll kick in fifty cents for every dollar you contribute, up to a cap. Or a full dollar-for-dollar match, up to some percentage of your salary. The specifics vary wildly. I've seen matches as good as dollar-for-dollar on the first six percent of salary, and as stingy as twenty-five cents per dollar on the first three percent. But the principle is always the same: you contribute, they contribute. Your account balance goes up by more than you actually put in.

It is—and I want to be extremely clear about this—free money. As in, money they are offering to give you, with no strings attached other than you have to put in some of your own money first.

If you are not contributing enough to get the full match, you are leaving cash on the ground and walking past it every two weeks.

Let me be viscerally specific about what that looks like, because I don't think the loss registers for most people until you spell it out in concrete terms.

You make seventy thousand a year. Your employer matches fifty percent of your contributions, up to six percent of your salary. If you contribute the full six percent—that's forty-two hundred dollars annually—they'll add another twenty-one hundred. Total going into your account: sixty-three hundred.

But right now you're only contributing three percent. Twenty-one hundred a year. They match half of that: ten-fifty. Which means you are missing out on the other ten-fifty they would have given you if you'd just logged into the benefits portal and changed one number from three to six.

One thousand fifty dollars. Every single year. Free. And you're not taking it.

Over ten years, that's ten thousand five hundred in matching contributions you didn't claim. And that's just the contributions themselves. Invested at a seven percent annual return—again, conservative for a stock-heavy portfolio over a decade—that ten-five would've grown to around fourteen thousand five hundred.

You have lost fourteen thousand five hundred dollars because you didn't spend five minutes updating a form.

But here's what that fourteen thousand five hundred actually represents, and this is the part that keeps me up at night when I think about how many people are doing this exact thing right now. Fourteen-five isn't just an abstract number on a statement. It's three months of rent. It's a used car that runs. It's a down payment on a bigger emergency fund, or a chunk of your kid's college tuition, or the difference between retiring at sixty-five and retiring at sixty-seven. It's real, tangible security that you traded for… what? The inconvenience of logging into a website?

I know what you're thinking, because I've heard it a dozen times: "I can't afford to contribute more. I'm barely making it as it is."

Sometimes that's true. Budgets are genuinely tight. There are people for whom an extra hundred bucks a month in take-home pay is the difference between paying rent on time and not. I'm not talking to those people right now. If that's you, if you're genuinely living paycheck-to-paycheck with no discretionary spending to cut, then fine. You've got bigger problems than optimizing your 401(k).

But for most people, when they actually sit down and track where money is going—and I mean really track it, every dollar, for a full month—they find room. Not unlimited room. Not enough to max out a 401(k) at twenty-three thousand a year. But enough to at least grab *some* of the match.

Two streaming services you forgot you were subscribed to. Eating out one less time per week. Buying the store brand instead of the name brand on things that taste identical. Skipping the daily coffee shop run and making it at home. I'm not saying live like a monk. I'm saying most people have at least fifty or a hundred dollars a month of spending that's more habitual than intentional, and redirecting that toward something that will compound for thirty years instead of evaporating into nothing is not deprivation. It's just being awake.

But here's what I've noticed, and it bothers me more than the money itself: I've had this exact conversation with people—shown them the math, made it crystal clear they're walking away from thousands of dollars—and they still don't increase their contribution. Not because they can't afford it. Because logging into the HR portal is annoying. Because they don't remember their password. Because the website interface is from 2009 and navigating it feels like doing homework.

The friction is barely real, but it's enough. And the system is fine with that. The system is designed to let you fail passively. Nobody's going to call you. Nobody's going to send you a letter saying, "Hey, you're leaving money on the table." The default is inertia, and inertia costs you thousands of dollars a year.

So if you take one thing from this chapter—forget the traditional-versus-Roth calculus, forget the compound interest projections, forget everything else—it's this: find out what your employer match is. It's in your benefits documents, or on the HR portal, or you can email someone and ask. Find out the percentage you need to contribute to get the full match. Then contribute that percentage.

If you're already doing that, great. You've cleared the lowest bar. Now the question is whether you can go higher, because the contribution limits on 401(k)s are high enough that if you can afford to push past the match and keep going, you're building serious wealth on a tax-deferred basis. Every dollar you put in above the match is still a dollar the IRS doesn't touch this year. Still a dollar that compounds without getting skimmed.

But the match comes first. Always. Because it's the only guaranteed return you're ever going to get. The market might go up, might go down. Your stock picks might pan out or they might crater. But a dollar-for-dollar match? That's an instant one hundred percent return, risk-free, the moment the money hits your account.

And if you're sitting there thinking, "Okay, fine, I'll do it, I'll bump my contribution up when I get a chance," let me stop you right there. Not when you get a chance. Now. This afternoon. Before you do anything else. Because "when I get a chance" turns into next week, turns into next month, turns into another year of walking past free money.

I'm not exaggerating when I say this is the single highest-return move most people can make with their money. Higher than picking the right stocks. Higher than timing the market. Higher than refinancing your mortgage at the perfect moment. You are being handed free money by your employer, and all you have to do is fill out a form.

The tax code isn't designed to minimize what you owe. It's designed to collect the maximum you'll tolerate without pushing back. Every deduction, every credit, every adjustment exists because someone fought for it, and if you don't claim it, the IRS certainly won't remind you. Retirement contributions are the clearest example of this. The system is structured to reward you for saving, because it's cheaper for the government than the alternative. But the reward doesn't just show up. You have to claim it.

So claim it.

Max out the match. Then, if you can, go higher. Contribute to an IRA—traditional or Roth, whichever fits your situation better, or split it if you're not sure. Every dollar you route through a retirement account is a dollar the IRS doesn't get to touch right now, and over the span of decades, that adds up to a difference that's not just meaningful but genuinely life-changing.

You can keep handing the government more than you owe, or you can start putting up a shield. The tax code's already written the rules. The accounts are already set up. The match is already being offered. All that's left is for you to do something about it.

And once you've done that—once you've actually got money sitting in these accounts, compounding away, shielded from taxes—the next question becomes: what do you do when some of those investments inevitably lose money? Because they will. The market doesn't go up in a straight line. Things drop. Positions go red. And when that happens, most people just sit there and watch, maybe feel a little sick about it, and wait for it to recover.

But there's a move you can make when your investments lose value. A move that turns the loss into something useful. Something that cuts your tax bill even further.

We'll get to that.

Free money is rare. But if you're going to lose money anyway—and you will, eventually—there's a way to make it count.

Chapter 5: Tax-Loss Harvesting Basics: Turning Losses into Gains

The letter arrived on a Thursday. Standard envelope, IRS return address in the corner, the kind of thing that makes your stomach drop before you even open it.

My friend Daniel—high school math teacher, two kids, sensible car, sensible mortgage—sat at his kitchen table staring at it for probably twenty minutes before he finally tore it open. He already knew what it was going to say. He'd made a gain selling some stock the previous year. About twelve thousand dollars. He'd reported it. Paid the tax. Filed on time. Everything by the book.

What he didn't know—what nobody had told him—was that he'd also been sitting on seventeen thousand dollars in losses from other investments he'd sold. Losses he never claimed. Because he didn't know he could.

The IRS wasn't writing to remind him of that opportunity, of course. They were writing to confirm receipt of his payment.

Daniel called me that night. "I just paid taxes on money I didn't actually make," he said. "How is that even legal?"

It's legal because the system assumes you know the rules. And if you don't? That's not the IRS's problem.

The tax code isn't designed to minimize what you owe—it's designed to collect the maximum you'll tolerate without pushing back. Every deduction exists because someone fought for it. And if you don't claim it, the IRS certainly won't remind you.

Tax-loss harvesting is one of those things that sounds like insider baseball. But it's not complicated. You sell an investment at a loss. You use that loss to offset gains you made elsewhere. If you don't have gains, you can deduct up to three thousand dollars of that loss against your regular income. Every year. And if you have more than three thousand in losses? They carry forward. Next year, the year after that, for as long as it takes.

Simple. Which is probably why most people never bother.

Here's the thing: this one actually pays you. This one puts money back in your pocket. And all it requires is that you pay attention once a year and make a decision.

When you sell something—stock, mutual fund, bond, whatever—you're creating either a capital gain or a capital loss. The IRS taxes gains. But they also let you use losses to offset those gains. Not out of generosity—out of structural necessity, because that's how capital markets work.

There's a split here that matters: short-term versus long-term. If you owned the asset for a year or less, it's short-term. More than a year, it's long-term. Short-term gains get taxed at your ordinary income rate—same brutal rate as your paycheck. Long-term gains get taxed lower. Zero, fifteen, or twenty percent depending on your income bracket.

Losses follow the same categories. Short-term losses offset short-term gains first. Long-term losses offset long-term gains first. Leftovers can cross over. And if you still have losses after everything cancels out? That's when the three-thousand-dollar deduction against ordinary income kicks in, with the remainder rolling forward to next year.

It's like a ledger. Red on one side, black on the other. You're just balancing the columns.

I remember sitting in my own office last November, staring at a spreadsheet of renewable energy startups I'd bought into back in 2018. A lot of promise. A lot of hype. Some genuinely good ideas, I still think. But the market didn't care about good ideas. It cared about profitability, and most of these companies weren't profitable. Probably never would be.

I'd been avoiding looking at this part of my portfolio for months. The longer you wait, the worse you expect it to be, and the worse you expect it to be, the harder it is to actually look. But I finally forced myself to pull the numbers. It was bad. The kind of painful that makes you question your entire investment philosophy.

That's when it shifted for me, though. Staring at all that red, I realized: this isn't just loss. It's potential. It's a tax benefit I can actually use. I had gains elsewhere in my portfolio—stuff I'd sold earlier in the year. And these losses could offset those gains. Dollar for dollar.

Turn something painful into something useful. Not because you're gaming the system. Because you're finally engaging with it.

Here's a scenario. Couple in their sixties, retired, living off Social Security and investment income. They sold some stock the previous year—long-term hold, made about eight thousand in gains. But they also owned a bond fund that got hammered during the rate hikes. Down six thousand. They sold it in November to cut their losses and reallocate.

Because they harvested those losses—offsetting the long-term gain with the long-term loss—their taxable income for the year dropped. They didn't pay zero tax. But they paid a hell of a lot less than they would have if they'd just sat on the bond fund, hoping it would recover.

That's the move. You're not trying to eliminate taxes altogether. You're trying to stop paying tax on phantom gains—gains that got wiped out by losses you absorbed elsewhere.

But you can't just sell everything that's down and call it a day. You'd be making investment decisions based on tax strategy instead of whether the investment is actually good. The goal is to harvest losses strategically. Without wrecking your long-term plan. You're pulling weeds, not scorching the earth.

Which brings us to the wash sale rule.

The IRS doesn't want you selling a stock at a loss just to claim the deduction and then buying it right back the next day. So they built in a thirty-day rule. If you sell an asset at a loss and then buy the same asset—or something "substantially identical"—within thirty days before or after the sale, you can't claim the loss. It doesn't vanish. It gets added to the cost basis of the replacement shares. But you don't get it now.

"Substantially identical" is where it gets messy. It's not just about buying the exact same ticker symbol. It's about functional equivalence. If you sell shares of an S&P; 500 index fund and immediately buy a different S&P; 500 index fund that tracks the exact same index, the IRS is probably going to call that substantially identical. But if you sell a tech-heavy ETF and buy a broader market ETF? That's different enough. You've changed your exposure.

I knew a young attorney once—brilliant guy, meticulous to a fault—who sold some stock at a loss in December thinking he was being clever. Two weeks later he bought it back because he still believed in the company. Completely reasonable. Except the IRS flagged it as a wash sale and disallowed the deduction.

He was furious. "I thought I was following the rules," he said.

"You were," I told him. "You just didn't know all of them."

The rules are there. They're not hidden. But nobody teaches you this stuff unless you go looking for it. And most people don't go looking until they've already made the mistake.

So how do you actually do this without screwing it up?

Once a year—I do it in late November, early December—you sit down and run what I call an Annual Loss Scan. You're not day-trading. You're not trying to time the market. You're just looking at your portfolio with clear eyes and asking: where am I down, and does it make sense to harvest any of these losses?

Pull up your brokerage account. Most platforms will show you unrealized gains and losses—the profit or loss you'd have if you sold right now. Look at everything in the red.

Then ask: do I still believe in this investment?

If yes—if you think the company's solid, the fund will recover, the fundamentals are sound—then decide whether you're willing to sell it now, take the tax loss, and either wait thirty-one days to buy it back or buy something similar but not identical. If you're not willing to be out of the position and you can't find a good substitute, don't sell. The tax benefit isn't worth abandoning an investment you believe in.

If no—if you've lost confidence, if the story's changed, if you're holding on out of pride or stubbornness—then sell. Take the loss. Move on. You were going to sell eventually anyway. Might as well get the tax benefit while you're at it.

I worked with a retired teacher a few years back. She'd built a conservative portfolio over thirty-some years. Rarely touched it. When we finally sat down together, she had several positions that were deep underwater, including a legacy tech company that hadn't innovated since the early 2000s and probably never would again.

She didn't want to sell. "It feels like admitting I made a mistake," she said.

"Everyone makes mistakes," I told her. "The question is what you do about them."

We talked through the numbers. The tax benefit of harvesting those losses. How it could offset capital gains. How it could reduce her ordinary income. But more than that, we talked about opportunity cost. That money was sitting there doing nothing. Dead weight. It could be reallocated into something with actual growth potential.

After a lot of back-and-forth, she agreed to sell. When we calculated the tax savings—a little over two thousand dollars—she actually smiled.

"That's a weekend getaway," she said. "I think I've earned it."

She had.

Pride kills a lot of smart financial moves. Pride is expensive. That stock you bought because you believed in the vision, the one that's down 40% and shows no sign of recovering? It's not just dead money.

It's a potential refund sitting there. But only if you claim it. Only if you're willing to admit the bet didn't work out and move on.

Most people can't do that. They cling to hope. They tell themselves it's not a loss until they sell. Which is technically true in accounting terms but absolutely false in practical reality. You've already lost the money. Selling just makes it official. And making it official is what unlocks the tax benefit.

The loss already happened. That's done. You can't change it. But you can still extract value from it by using it to reduce your tax bill. You're not pretending the loss didn't hurt. You're acknowledging it, quantifying it, and then turning it into something else. A credit against gains. A deduction against income. A small shield against a system that's otherwise entirely focused on taking.

I had a client once—retired accountant, which makes this even more absurd—who held onto a failing pharmaceutical stock for five years because he was convinced it was "due for a turnaround." Lost a fortune. Not just the original investment. But also the thousands in tax deductions he could've claimed if he'd just cut his losses earlier.

When I asked him why he didn't sell, he said, "It felt like admitting defeat."

I told him it felt more like throwing good money after bad.

You can't control the market. You can't predict whether something will recover or continue tanking. But you can control whether you claim the tax benefit from losses you've already absorbed. The IRS will tax your gains every single time. They'll take their cut without hesitation. But they won't remind you to offset those gains with your losses. That's on you.

And if you don't do it, you're leaving money on the table. Not hypothetical future money. Real, immediate tax savings that could go into your pocket instead of theirs.

What serves you is action. Looking at those losses, making a rational decision about whether the investment is still worth holding, and then—if it's not—harvesting the loss and moving forward. Not dwelling. Not beating yourself up. Just moving forward with the knowledge that you've reclaimed some value from a bad situation.

That's what this is really about. Not a loophole. Not a trick. Just a recognition that losses happen, and when they do, you might as well get something out of them.

So before the year ends, pull up your brokerage account. Look at what's down. Ask yourself whether you still believe in those investments. And if you don't—if the story's changed, if you've lost faith, if you're holding on out of sheer stubbornness—sell. Claim the loss. Take the deduction.

Because the system isn't neutral. It's not designed to help you. It's designed to collect. And every year you don't harvest losses, every year you let pride or inertia or wishful thinking keep you from claiming what's yours, you're funding that collection system with money you didn't have to give.

Daniel's still mad about that letter, by the way. Not at the IRS. At himself. For not knowing better. For not asking. For assuming someone would've told him if there was a benefit he was missing.

But nobody tells you. That's the point. You have to know to look.

And now you do.

The letter arrived on a Thursday. Standard envelope, IRS return address in the corner, the kind of thing that makes your stomach drop before you even open it.

Daniel turned a twelve-thousand-dollar loss into a tax benefit he could use for years. What he still didn't know: he'd missed a three-thousand-dollar credit that would have landed as cash in his account within weeks.

Chapter 6: Credits You Might Be Missing: Beyond the Standard

The question came up in March, three years ago, while I was sitting at my kitchen table helping a friend file her taxes. She worked from home—freelance graphic design, clients scattered across the country, all of it coordinated from a laptop balanced between cookbooks and a perpetually half-empty coffee mug.

For three years, I'd been Buffett's secretary—taking the standard deduction, moving on with my life. The home office deduction was sitting there the whole time. I just hadn't known to claim it.

She mentioned, casually, that her accountant had told her to claim the home office deduction. I remember stopping mid-sentence, staring at her setup. The laptop. The stack of papers. The charging cable snaking across the table to a wall outlet behind the refrigerator. This was her qualifying space?

I had a corner in my bedroom. An actual desk, wedged between the bed and a laundry basket that never quite emptied. I did freelance work there on weekends and evenings—writing, editing, consulting projects that paid the bills when my main job didn't stretch far enough. I'd been doing it for three years. Regular. Consistent. Exclusive use of that space for business.

And I'd never claimed it. Not once.

I'd convinced myself the deduction was for people with *real* home offices. Separate rooms. Dedicated entrances. Professional setups. People whose businesses looked like businesses, not someone like me squeezing side work into the margins of a regular life.

That night, I looked up the rules. Square footage used regularly and exclusively for business, multiplied by the prescribed rate. Simple math. I qualified. I'd qualified the whole time. Roughly $2,100 over three years, left on the table because I'd never questioned my own assumption about who the deduction was *for*.

It wasn't the money that bothered me most, though $2,100 would have made a difference. It was the realization that I'd been operating under a set of beliefs about the tax code—beliefs I'd never examined, never tested—and those beliefs had cost me. The IRS hadn't reminded me. The tax software hadn't flagged it. I'd filed my returns, gotten my refunds, moved on. And the system had quietly kept what I didn't know to ask for.

That's the structure we're working within. The tax code isn't designed to minimize what you owe. It's designed to collect the maximum you'll tolerate without pushing back. Every deduction, every credit, every adjustment exists because someone fought for it—a lobby, a coalition, a compromise hammered out in some legislative backroom. But claiming it? That's on you. And if you don't, the IRS certainly won't send a reminder.

I know this sounds adversarial, like I'm framing the IRS as some kind of predator waiting to pounce. That's not quite it. It's structural. The system isn't actively trying to deceive you, but it's also not working to ensure you claim everything you're entitled to. It's neutral in a way that benefits the default outcome: you pay what you file, and if you leave money on the table, that's your business.

Most people do leave money on the table. Not because they're careless—though some are—but because they assume certain credits don't apply to them. They see a question on their tax software about education expenses and think, *I'm not in college, so this doesn't matter.* They see a mention of the Child and Dependent Care Credit and skip it because they're not sure if their after-school program counts. They contribute to a retirement account and never realize there's a credit specifically designed to reward them for doing so.

The pattern is always the same: a quiet assumption that the credit is for *someone else*. Someone with more complicated finances. Someone who knows the system better. Someone poorer, or richer, or just… different. And so they don't ask. They don't dig into the forms. They file, accept the refund, move on.

And the IRS keeps the difference.

Let me show you what that looks like in practice.

Karen Chen spent eleven thousand dollars on daycare last year. Not a nice-to-have expense—*necessary* expense so she could work full-time as a marketing coordinator while her partner managed a sales route that kept him on the road three days a week. Their daughter was four. The daycare was a no-frills operation in a church basement, staffed by two women who'd been running it for fifteen years. It smelled like graham crackers and disinfectant. It cost $900 a month.

Karen kept every receipt. She had a system: labeled envelopes, one for each month, tucked into a drawer in the kitchen. January through December, all accounted for. When tax season came around, she pulled them out, proud of her organization, ready to claim… something. She wasn't sure what, exactly, but surely daycare expenses mattered.

Her tax software asked about dependent care expenses. She entered the eleven thousand. The software calculated a credit. She assumed it was correct, clicked through the remaining screens, filed the return. Got her refund a couple weeks later—about $1,200—and felt relieved that tax season was over.

What she didn't realize until the following year, when she mentioned her process to a coworker, was that the software had capped her credit at a much lower amount than she could have claimed. The Child and Dependent Care Credit allows you to claim a percentage of your expenses—up to $3,000 for one qualifying child, $6,000 for two or more. The percentage depends on your income, ranging from 20% to 35%.

Karen's income put her at the 30% rate. She could have claimed 30% of $3,000—the maximum for one child. That's $900.

But the software, in its default configuration, had used a different set of numbers. She'd missed about $300 in credit. Not because the software was wrong—it calculated based on the information she gave it—but because she hadn't understood the limits, the percentages, the way the credit actually worked. She'd trusted the automation and assumed it would maximize her benefit.

It didn't. It couldn't. It only knew what she told it.

The following year, Karen also contributed $3,500 to her 401(k). Not a huge amount, but more than she'd managed the year before, and she felt good about it—responsible, forward-thinking, doing what you're supposed to do when you're in your mid-thirties and starting to worry about retirement.

She didn't know about the Saver's Credit. Officially called the Retirement Savings Contributions Credit, it's designed to reward lower- and moderate-income taxpayers for contributing to retirement accounts. The credit can be 10%, 20%, or 50% of your contribution, depending on your income, up to a maximum contribution amount of

$2,000 for single filers or $4,000 for married couples filing jointly.

Karen and her partner filed jointly. Their combined income put them at the 20% rate. They could have claimed 20% of $4,000 in combined contributions—$800.

They contributed $3,500 between them. Twenty percent of $3,500 is $700.

Karen had no idea this existed. She filed her return, answered the questions about retirement contributions for the deduction—because she knew contributions to a traditional 401(k) reduce your taxable income—but never saw the question about the Saver's Credit. Or maybe she saw it and didn't understand it. Or maybe the software didn't surface it clearly because it didn't have enough information to flag it as relevant.

Add the missed $300 from the dependent care credit and the $700 from the Saver's Credit, and Karen left $1,000 on the table that year. A thousand dollars that could have padded their emergency fund, knocked down the credit card balance lingering from the previous year's car repair, or just… eased things. Made life a little less tight.

She filed on time. Kept good records. Did everything she thought she was supposed to do. And the system quietly kept what she didn't know to claim.

You might be thinking this is an edge case, that most people don't qualify for multiple credits at once. You'd be wrong. The broader your financial life—kids, education, retirement contributions, work-related expenses—the more likely it is you're leaving something unclaimed. And even one missed credit, compounded over years, adds up to real money.

The Lifetime Learning Credit is one people miss constantly. They assume education credits are only for college students paying tuition. Wrong. This credit covers courses taken to acquire or improve job skills, whether or not you're pursuing a degree. Professional certifications. Industry workshops. A single online course meant to make you more competitive in your field.

You can claim 20% of the first $10,000 in qualified education expenses—up to $2,000 per year. There are income limits. For 2023, it phases out for single filers with modified adjusted gross income between $80,000 and $90,000, and for married couples filing jointly between $160,000 and $180,000. But if you're below those thresholds and you paid for work-related education last year, this is real money sitting unclaimed.

Maria Rodriguez is a paralegal in Phoenix. Single mother, one kid, works full-time at a mid-sized law firm doing document review, client intake, the kind of steady but unglamorous work that keeps the wheels turning. Last year she spent $800 on an online legal technology certification. Not because she was plotting a career change, but because she wanted a raise—or at least wanted to make herself more valuable in case she needed to jump to another firm in a tight market.

The course taught her how to use e-discovery software, case management systems, the digital tools that are increasingly non-negotiable in legal work. She paid for it on a credit card, completed it over three months of late nights after her son went to bed, added it to her resume.

When tax season came, she didn't think of it as a tax event. She thought of it as a career investment, the kind of thing you do because every career advice article tells you to "keep learning" and "stay competitive." Her tax software asked about education expenses, but the questions seemed oriented toward traditional college costs—1098-T forms, degree programs, tuition bills. She didn't have any of that, so she clicked past.

If she'd known, she could have claimed $160. Twenty percent of $800. Not a fortune. But enough to cover a week of groceries, or a tank of gas, or a small dent in the credit card balance that never quite went away.

And that's just one credit.

Maria also spent $3,500 on after-school care for her eight-year-old son. He got out of school at three. She didn't get off work until six. The program wasn't fancy—just a local community center that kept kids busy with homework help and recreational activities—but it cost her $300 a month during the school year. She paid it out of her checking account, filed the receipts in a drawer at home because it seemed like the responsible thing to do, and never connected it to her taxes.

That qualifies for the Child and Dependent Care Credit. The same one Karen used, though Maria could have claimed a higher percentage based on her income. Let's say she qualifies for 30%. Her $3,500 in expenses hit the $3,000 cap for one child, so she'd calculate 30% of $3,000. That's $900.

Maria also contributed $2,000 to a traditional IRA. She set up an automatic transfer from her checking account—$167 a month—and mostly forgot about it. By the end of the year, she'd saved $2,000 without feeling the individual withdrawals, which was the whole point.

That contribution makes her eligible for the Saver's Credit. If her income qualifies her for the 50% rate, she'd get $1,000—50% of her $2,000 contribution, up to the maximum.

Add it up: $160 from the Lifetime Learning Credit, $900 from the Child and Dependent Care Credit, $1,000 from the Saver's Credit. That's $2,060 in credits she's entitled to. Money that comes directly off her tax bill, dollar for dollar.

If Maria owes $2,500 in federal taxes after withholding and claims these credits, her bill drops to $440. If she's already had $2,800 withheld through payroll, she goes from expecting a $300 refund to getting back $2,360.

That's the difference between barely scraping by and having a cushion. That's the difference between putting an emergency car repair on a credit card at 22% interest and paying cash. That's the difference between stress and breathing room.

Maria didn't claim any of it. She filed her return using free online software, answered the questions as best she could, got her small refund, moved on. She'll probably do the same thing this year unless something changes.

Not because she's irresponsible. She's working full-time, raising a kid on her own, saving for retirement despite not having much margin. She's doing everything right except one thing: she's not claiming what's hers.

And the system isn't set up to remind her.

Here's what bothers me about all of this: it's not that the tax code is hiding these credits. The information is publicly available. The IRS publishes guides. Tax software includes the questions. It's just that the burden is entirely on you to know what to look for, to recognize when something applies to your situation, to ask the right questions in the right order.

It's a passive system that rewards knowledge and penalizes ignorance. And most people are operating with incomplete knowledge—not because they're lazy or stupid, but because they're busy, overwhelmed, and trying to get through tax season as quickly as possible without making a costly mistake.

So they play it safe. They stick to the basics. They claim what's obvious and skip what's uncertain. And the IRS is perfectly content with that outcome.

Credits are fundamentally different from deductions, and understanding that difference matters more than most people realize. A deduction reduces your taxable income. If you're in the 24% tax bracket and you take a $1,000 deduction, you save $240 in taxes. Useful, certainly. But a $1,000 credit? That's a dollar-for-dollar reduction in what you owe. The full thousand comes directly off your tax bill.

You can see why credits are more valuable. You can also see why it's worth understanding which ones you qualify for.

The Earned Income Tax Credit—EITC—is the big one people miss, mostly because they assume they make too much money to qualify. It's aimed at low- to moderate-income workers and families, and the income limits are higher than most people think. For 2023, a single parent with two kids could have an adjusted gross income up to about $56,000 and still qualify for some amount of the credit. The maximum credit for that scenario is over $6,000.

Six thousand dollars.

And it's refundable, which means even if your tax liability is zero—if you don't owe anything after withholding—you can still get the credit as a refund. It's not a loan. It's not an advance. It's money the tax code says you're entitled to because your income falls within a certain range and you meet the other requirements.

David is a construction worker in North Carolina. Thirty-two years old, unmarried, no kids. He earned about $31,000 last year doing framing work for a residential contractor. Long days in the heat, physical labor that left him sore most nights. His income came through a W-2, so taxes were withheld from every paycheck. When tax season rolled around, he filed a basic return, claimed the standard deduction, figured he'd get back whatever had been over-withheld.

He didn't realize he qualified for the EITC. He thought it was only for people with children—single mothers, struggling families, people in worse shape than him. The acronym sounded like a welfare program, something he didn't need and didn't want to ask for.

He was wrong. Single workers without kids can qualify too, though the credit amount is smaller. For 2023, a single filer without children could earn up to about $17,640 and qualify for a maximum credit of around $600. David earned too much to qualify at that income level—but if he'd been just under that threshold, or if his circumstances had been slightly different, he'd have been leaving money unclaimed because of an assumption.

And plenty of people *with* children miss it entirely. They see the questions, don't understand the income limits, assume they're disqualified, and move on. Or they're intimidated by the form—Schedule EIC—and decide it's not worth the hassle.

The IRS estimates that about 20% of eligible taxpayers don't claim the EITC. Twenty percent. Millions of people, leaving billions of dollars unclaimed, mostly because they don't know they qualify or they're afraid of making a mistake.

That's the cost of inaction. Not dramatic. Not a crisis. Just a steady leak of money you'll never get back because you didn't ask the question.

I know what you're thinking: this sounds exhausting. Sifting through tax forms, chasing down credits, calculating eligibility requirements—it feels like a second job on top of your actual job. And honestly? Sometimes it is. It *is* work. It requires effort, attention, a willingness to dig into details that feel tedious and bureaucratic.

But compare that temporary inconvenience to the alternative: leaving money on the table year after year, effectively gifting it to a system that isn't actively working to return it to you. It's not about getting a bigger refund. It's about keeping what you already earned. Money that could ease pressure, build a buffer, give you options.

Sarah Jenkins is a high school English teacher outside Atlanta. Fifteen years in the classroom, a solid career with decent benefits but a paycheck that never quite stretched as far as it needed to. Two kids in private school—a choice she and her husband made years ago and couldn't easily reverse—plus a mortgage, car payments, the usual pile of expenses that accumulate when you're raising a family.

Last year she spent over $5,000 on tuition. Another $800 on extracurricular activities—soccer fees, debate club registration, piano lessons. Nearly $1,200 on classroom supplies for her students, because the school's budget didn't cover the books and materials she wanted to use. She bought most of it on a credit card, racked up interest every month because she didn't have the cash flow to pay it off immediately.

She filed her taxes using TurboTax. Answered the questions. Got a refund of about $900. It felt like a small win—extra money she hadn't been counting on, enough to knock down part of the credit card balance.

What she didn't realize was that some of those classroom expenses might have qualified for a deduction. The IRS allows educators to deduct up to $300 in unreimbursed expenses for classroom supplies—books, software, materials you buy with your own money for your students. It's not a credit; it's an above-the-line deduction, which means you can claim it even if you take the standard deduction.

Sarah spent $1,200. She could have deducted $300. If she's in the 22% tax bracket, that's $66 in tax savings. Not huge, but real. And she missed it entirely because she didn't know it existed.

She also didn't realize that her kids' extracurricular expenses might qualify for the Child and Dependent Care Credit if the activities happened while she and her husband were working. Summer camps, after-school programs—if you're paying for supervision so you can work, it often counts.

The tuition itself? That's trickier. Education expenses for K-12 aren't generally creditable the way college expenses are, though there are exceptions depending on your state and whether the school qualifies as a special-needs program. But the point is, Sarah didn't even investigate. She assumed private school tuition was just a cost she had to absorb, unconnected to her taxes.

Maybe she was right. Maybe none of it would have qualified under closer scrutiny. But she didn't ask. She didn't dig into the rules. She filed her return, took the refund the software calculated, and moved on.

And if there was money left on the table—$66 here, $200 there—she'll never know.

That's the quiet cost. Not a single catastrophic mistake, but a series of small missed opportunities that add up over time. A few hundred dollars this year, a few hundred next year, compounding into thousands over a decade. Money that could have built an emergency fund, paid down debt, funded a vacation, smoothed out the rough edges of a tight budget.

The tax code isn't going to meet you halfway. It's not designed to. Every credit, every deduction, every break exists because someone lobbied for it, but the system doesn't actively ensure you claim it. It's structured to collect what you file, and if you file less than you're entitled to, that's your loss.

I'm not saying this to make you paranoid or to suggest you need to spend hours poring over IRS publications every year. But I am saying it's worth questioning your assumptions. It's worth asking, *What might I be missing?* It's worth taking an extra hour to dig into the credits that *might* apply to you, rather than skipping them because you assume they don't.

Because the alternative is this: you keep doing everything you think you're supposed to do—filing on time, keeping records, answering the questions—and the system keeps what you don't claim. Not maliciously. Not vindictively. Just… structurally. And the gap between what you owe and what you pay stays wider than it needs to be.

Here's a simple framework to start closing that gap.

First, map your financial life into categories the tax code cares about. Education expenses—yours or your kids'. Childcare or dependent care costs. Retirement contributions. Work-related expenses you paid out of pocket. Anything you spent money on that relates to earning income, improving your skills, or supporting your ability to work.

Second, for each category, look up the relevant credit or deduction. You don't need to memorize the tax code. You just need to know what questions to ask. Did you pay for work-related courses? Look up the Lifetime Learning Credit. Did you pay for daycare or after-school care? Look up the Child and Dependent Care Credit. Did you contribute to an IRA or 401(k)? Look up the Saver's Credit.

Third, don't assume you're disqualified. Income limits exist, but they're often higher than people think. Eligibility requirements can be specific, but they're not as narrow as they seem. Read the rules. Check the thresholds. If you're close, dig deeper. If you're uncertain, ask someone—a tax professional, a knowledgeable friend, even the IRS helpline if you're patient enough.

Fourth, document everything. Not just for the credits you're sure about, but for the ones you're investigating. Keep receipts. Note dates, amounts, what the expense was for. If you're audited—unlikely, but possible—you'll need to back up your claims. And even if you're never audited, the act of documenting forces you to think clearly about what qualifies.

Fifth, revisit this every year. Your financial life changes. Your income shifts. Your family situation evolves. A credit you didn't qualify for last year might be available this year. An expense you've been paying for years might suddenly cross a threshold that makes it worth claiming. Don't assume this year is the same as last year and file the same way out of habit.

This isn't about gaming the system. It's not about pushing boundaries or claiming things you're not entitled to. It's about engaging with the tax code as it actually exists, rather than as you assume it exists. It's about recognizing that the system is passive, that it won't come looking for you, and that if you want to keep what's yours, you have to claim it.

Most people don't. They assume the software will catch it, or that credits are for someone else, or that the effort isn't worth the return. And so they leave money on the table. Not once, but year after year, building a quiet deficit they'll never recover.

You don't have to be one of them.

Start with one credit. Just one. Pick the one that seems most likely to apply to your situation—the one where you have expenses and income in the right range. Dig into the rules. Figure out if you qualify. If you do, claim it. If you don't, move to the next one.

Next year, add another. The year after that, another. Build the habit of asking, *What am I missing?* Build the reflex to question your assumptions, to look beyond the obvious, to engage with the parts of the tax code that work in your favor.

Because here's the truth most people don't want to hear: the IRS isn't your adversary, but it's not your ally either. It's a system. It collects what you file. It processes what you submit. It doesn't care if you leave money on the table, because that money just stays in the general fund. It doesn't care if you overpay, because overpayment is just an interest-free loan you're giving the government.

The only person who cares about keeping your money is you. And if you don't claim it, no one else will.

Michelle spent six hours reconstructing her year from bank statements. The credits were there. She just couldn't prove them.

Chapter 7: The Year-Round Tax Tracker: Building the Habit

You're going to spend six hours in March reconstructing your entire financial year from bank statements and fading memory. You know this. You do it every year. What if I told you there's a way to make those six hours disappear—and it takes fifteen minutes a month?

"Was it the tutoring for my son?" she asked me, almost pleading. "Or was that the month I bought the patio furniture?"

I didn't have the answer. Neither did she. And here's the thing—it probably *was* the tutoring, which would've been deductible if she could prove it. But she couldn't. So she didn't claim it. And the IRS, as you might imagine, didn't send her a helpful reminder.

This happens all the time. Not just with Michelle, but with nearly everyone I meet. Smart people, organized people, people who run businesses and manage teams and remember birthdays and never miss a dentist appointment. And yet, come tax season, they're all doing the same frantic archaeology, digging through months of financial debris, hoping they don't miss something important.

You know what I'm talking about, don't you? That sinking feeling in March when you realize you should've been tracking things all year. The shoebox of receipts—some legible, some not. The vague sense that you're leaving money on the table, but you can't quite put your finger on where.

Here's what nobody tells you: the system is designed this way.

Not maliciously, necessarily. But structurally. The tax code isn't built to minimize what you owe—it's built to collect the maximum you'll tolerate without pushing back. Every deduction exists because someone fought for it. Every credit is there because a lobbyist argued for it, or a constituency demanded it, or a politician needed a win. And if you don't claim it? Well, the IRS isn't going to remind you. They're not your advocate. They're the collector.

This isn't about being adversarial. It's about being realistic. The government provides the mechanisms—deductions, credits, adjustments—but it's on *you* to use them. And if you don't engage with the system throughout the year, you lose by default.

The question isn't whether you *should* track your tax-relevant expenses. Of course you should. You already know that. You've told yourself a hundred times: "This year, I'm going to stay organized."

The question is: why doesn't it stick?

Because here's the truth—and I say this with all the empathy I can muster—it's not about information. You don't need another article explaining what's deductible. You need a habit. And habits, as it turns out, are harder to build than we'd like to admit.

Let me back up for a second and tell you about a report the IRS Inspector General released back in 2013. They estimated that roughly $1.3 billion in education credits went unclaimed each year. Not because people weren't eligible. Not because the rules were impossibly complex. But because most taxpayers simply didn't know the credits existed, or they forgot to track the qualifying expenses, or they lost the receipts by April.

$1.3 billion. Just sitting there. And that's *one* category of credits.

Medical expenses? Same story. Charitable contributions? Yep. Business expenses for side hustles? Absolutely. The pattern repeats across the board: people spend the money, they're entitled to the deduction, and then they... forget. Or they can't prove it. Or they don't realize it qualifies in the first place.

Michelle's tutoring expense is a perfect microcosm of this. She paid for it. She was entitled to claim it. But because she didn't track it at the time, and because she couldn't definitively prove it three months later, she left that money on the table. Multiply that across a year, across multiple categories, and you start to see how this adds up.

You're probably thinking, "Okay, but I don't have time for another system."

I know. You've got work deadlines, kids who need rides to practice, a home that always seems to need one more repair, maybe aging parents who need help. Your mental load is already maxed out. Adding one more thing—even a small thing—feels impossible.

But here's what I want you to consider: you're *already* spending time on this. Just not in a way that helps you.

Think about what actually happens when you don't track throughout the year. You spend hours—*hours*—in March and April trying to reconstruct everything. You dig through bank statements. You email your doctor's office asking for a printout of last year's payments (a request that always feels slightly embarrassing, doesn't it?). You guess at mileage because you didn't log it. You skip deductions entirely because you can't prove them.

That scattered, stressful work? It takes *way* more time than five minutes a week would have.

And the real cost isn't just time. It's the money you're leaving on the table, and the peace of mind you're sacrificing for no good reason.

Let me tell you about Tom.

Tom was a physical therapist who ran his own small practice outside of Boston. Good guy. Worked hard. Made decent money. Every year he'd show up to his accountant's office in early April with a manila envelope stuffed with receipts. Some were faded. Some were stained with coffee. Some were for things he couldn't quite remember.

"Was that a business lunch or just grabbing takeout?" he'd ask, shrugging.

His accountant, a woman named Susan with thirty years of experience navigating this labyrinth for small-business owners, would do her best. But there's only so much you can claim when the documentation is a mess.

One year, Susan sat him down and said, "You're probably leaving three, maybe four thousand dollars on the table every year, Tom. Not because you're not eligible. Because you can't prove it."

That got his attention.

Tom was a hands-on therapist. He knew the value of precision, of getting the details right. The idea that he was losing that kind of money simply due to disorganization—it stung.

So he tried something different. He didn't overhaul his entire life. He just set a reminder on his phone: every Sunday evening at 8 PM, review the week's expenses.

It took him about seven minutes.

He'd pull up his bank account on his phone, scroll through the transactions, and flag anything that might be business-related—continuing education courses, new equipment for the practice, even mileage between appointments. He'd snap a photo of any paper receipts he'd collected during the week and drop them in a folder on his phone labeled "2024 Tax Stuff."

That's it. Seven minutes. Once a week.

By the end of the year, Tom had a clear record. Susan was thrilled—she actually smiled when he handed her the organized file. And Tom got back about $3,400 more than he had the previous year. Not because he'd changed his spending. Because he'd actually *captured* what he was already entitled to claim.

Seven minutes a week. Call it six hours over the course of a year. That works out to roughly $567 per hour of his time, just for basic record-keeping.

Show me another investment that pays that kind of return.

But here's the thing about habits, though: they don't stick because of willpower.

Willpower is a terrible foundation. It runs out. You get tired, distracted, overwhelmed. If your system depends on you being disciplined and motivated every single week, it's going to fail. I've seen it a thousand times. Hell, I've *lived* it.

Habits stick when they're tied to something you already do, when the friction is low, and when the outcome feels tangible.

Think about flossing. (Stay with me here.) You know you're supposed to floss. Your dentist has been telling you this since you were eight. But most people don't floss daily because it's not tied to anything, it feels like extra work, and the benefit is distant and abstract.

But if you put the floss *right next* to your toothbrush, and you floss *immediately after* brushing (which you already do), and you notice after a few weeks that your gums bleed less—suddenly it's easier. It's attached to an existing routine. The friction is low. The benefit is noticeable.

Same principle applies here.

Don't try to carve out a brand-new block of time every week for "tax stuff." Attach it to something you already do. Maybe it's Sunday evening when you're reviewing your calendar for the week ahead. Maybe it's Friday afternoon when you're wrapping up work for the week. Maybe it's Wednesday during lunch.

Doesn't matter *when*. What matters is that it's consistent and linked to an existing anchor.

And don't aim for perfection. I'm not asking you to spend an hour every week doing detailed tax calculations. I'm asking you to spend five to ten minutes *capturing information*. That's it. You're not filing your return in July. You're just making sure that when April comes, you're not starting from zero.

Let me walk you through a simple system. I'm calling it the "Tax Tuesday" method, though you can call it whatever you want and do it on whatever day makes sense for you. The name doesn't matter. The consistency does.

Step one: Pick a day. Let's say Tuesday. Put a recurring reminder on your phone or calendar. Label it something simple—"Tax check-in" or "Receipt review" or just "Money." Make it recurring. Every single week. Non-negotiable.

Step two: When the reminder goes off, pull up your bank account or credit card statement. You're looking for anything from the past week that *might* be tax-relevant. Did you pay for childcare? Make a charitable donation? Buy supplies for a side business? Pay a medical bill? Contribute to an HSA or retirement account? Make an energy-efficient home improvement?

You don't need to know whether it's *definitely* deductible. You're not a tax attorney. You're just flagging possibilities.

Step three: Log it. This can be as simple as a spreadsheet with four columns: Date, Description, Amount, Category. Or you can use a notes app on your phone. Or a dedicated budgeting tool. The format doesn't matter. What matters is that you write it down *somewhere* consistent.

Step four: Grab the documentation. If there's a receipt, snap a photo with your phone. If it's an electronic transaction, save the confirmation email or download the statement. Drop everything into a folder—either physical or digital—labeled clearly. "2024 Tax Docs" or something similar. You're not organizing it perfectly. You're just making sure it exists in one place.

That's the whole system. Four steps. Five to ten minutes. Once a week.

Now, I know what you're thinking. "Okay, but what if I forget a week?"

You will. Life happens. Someone gets sick. You go on vacation. You have a brutal week at work and the last thing you want to do is think about taxes.

That's fine. Don't beat yourself up. Just pick it back up the next week.

The goal isn't perfection. The goal is *consistency over time*. Missing one week doesn't ruin the system. Missing ten weeks in a row means you don't actually have a system—you have a good intention that didn't stick.

If you find yourself consistently skipping it, that's feedback. Maybe Tuesday doesn't work. Maybe ten minutes feels like too much. Adjust. Try a different day. Cut it down to five minutes. The system should serve you, not the other way around.

I had a client—Rachel, a single mom with two kids and a full-time job—who tried this and kept skipping it. Not because she didn't care. Because Tuesday nights were chaos. Homework, dinner, baths, bedtime. By the time she had a free moment, it was 9:30 PM and she was too exhausted to think about receipts.

So we moved it to Saturday morning. She'd wake up, make coffee, and spend five minutes reviewing the week while the kids watched cartoons. That worked. It fit into her life instead of fighting against it.

The system doesn't have to look like Tom's. It doesn't have to look like Rachel's. It just has to work for *you*.

But let me acknowledge something else here, because I think it's important: this isn't just about the money.

I mean, yes, the money matters. Of course it does. Reclaiming a few thousand dollars a year is significant. But the real benefit—the thing that surprised me when I started doing this myself—is the sense of control.

Because here's what actually happens when you don't track throughout the year: you feel powerless. You feel like taxes are something that happen *to* you, not something you participate in. You feel like the system is rigged, and maybe it is, but you're not even trying to play the game.

And that feeling—that low-grade resentment, that sense of being perpetually behind, that anxiety that you've forgotten something important—it drains energy from everything else in your life.

I remember my grandfather, Leo. He was a carpenter his entire life. Built houses, furniture, everything by hand. A man who understood value, not just in dollars and cents, but in the effort it took to create something real.

He hated tax season. Not because he resented paying taxes—he was proud to contribute. But the *process* drove him crazy. The sorting through receipts, the deciphering forms, the constant second-guessing. It felt like an audit of his entire life. Like everything he'd worked for was being questioned.

He used to say, "It's not about the dollars, kiddo. It's about the principle."

And what he meant wasn't some abstract political statement. He meant that feeling of being powerless, of having to jump through hoops just to keep what was rightfully his.

I see a lot of that in my clients. The frustration. The resentment. The sense that they're playing a game rigged against them.

And honestly? They're not wrong.

The tax code *is* complicated by design. It's intentionally opaque, filled with loopholes and exceptions and arcane rules that benefit those who can afford to navigate it.

But that doesn't mean you have to be a victim of the system.

You just need to be proactive. You need to build a habit—a small, sustainable routine that protects your money and gives you peace of mind.

I'll be honest with you: even for me, building this habit wasn't easy.

For years, I was like so many of you. Good intentions. A shoebox full of receipts. A growing sense of dread as April loomed closer. I used to tell myself, "I'll get organized next year."

Next year never came.

The turning point happened when I realized the problem wasn't my lack of accounting skills—it was my timing. Trying to reconstruct an entire year's worth of financial activity in a few weeks is like trying to assemble a jigsaw puzzle with half the pieces missing, while someone keeps interrupting you and demanding updates.

It's stressful. It's inefficient. And it's almost guaranteed to result in errors.

So I started experimenting. Spreadsheets. Apps. Physical folders. I tried them all.

But nothing really stuck until I simplified it down to its core components: capture information regularly, document everything, and make it a habit.

The key wasn't finding the perfect system. It was making the system fit into my life, not the other way around.

I stopped trying to overhaul my entire financial routine and started with just five minutes a week. Five minutes to scan my bank account, flag potential deductions, and snap a photo of any paper receipts.

It felt almost ridiculously small at first. Like it couldn't possibly make a difference.

But that's the power of compounding. Small actions, repeated consistently over time, add up to remarkable results.

I started doing it on Sunday evenings while watching football—a mindless activity I already enjoyed. It wasn't about adding another task to my list. It was about replacing a passive one with an active one. Instead of mindlessly scrolling through social media, I was taking control of my finances.

And the results were immediate. Not in terms of huge tax savings—though those came later—but in terms of peace of mind.

Knowing that I had a handle on my expenses, that I wasn't going to be surprised by anything when April rolled around, lifted a weight off my shoulders.

I started feeling less anxious about money. More confident in my ability to manage it effectively.

And that, as you probably know, is priceless.

There's another layer to this, though, that I want to touch on. Because I think it gets at something deeper than just tax savings or peace of mind.

When you build a habit like this—when you consistently track your expenses, document your deductions, and stay organized throughout the year—you're not just protecting your money. You're reclaiming agency in a system that's designed to make you feel powerless.

Think about it. The tax code is thousands of pages long. It's written in language that's deliberately obscure. It changes every year. And unless you're a tax professional, you're expected to navigate it on your own, figure out what you owe, and hope you don't make a mistake that triggers an audit.

It's intimidating by design. And that intimidation serves a purpose: it makes you passive. It makes you accept whatever refund or bill you get without questioning it. It makes you feel grateful for a refund—even though, as we've discussed, a refund is just your own money being returned to you after you gave the government an interest-free loan.

But when you engage with the system proactively—when you track your expenses, claim your deductions, and refuse to leave money on the table—you're taking back control. You're saying, "I'm not going to let inertia dictate my financial fate."

And that shift in mindset, from passive recipient to active participant, changes everything.

Rachel, the single mom I mentioned earlier, put it this way: "Before I started doing this, tax season felt like giving money *away*. Like I was just passively letting the government take what they wanted. Now, it feels more... empowering. I'm actively claiming what's mine."

And that's exactly it. This isn't about gaming the system or finding loopholes. It's about knowing what you're entitled to and making sure you get it.

Let me give you another example, because I think it illustrates the broader principle at play here.

A few years ago, I had a client named David. He was an engineer, mid-forties, married with two kids. Made a solid six-figure income. By all accounts, he was financially stable.

But he had this nagging anxiety about taxes. Every year, he'd file his return and then spend the next few weeks second-guessing himself. Did he claim everything he was supposed to? Did he miss something? Was the IRS going to come knocking?

It wasn't rational. He'd never been audited. He had a good accountant. But the anxiety persisted.

We started digging into where that anxiety came from, and it turned out it wasn't really about taxes. It was about control—or rather, the lack of it.

David was someone who liked to understand how things worked. He was methodical, detail-oriented, the kind of person who reads the manual before assembling furniture. But when it came to taxes, he felt like he was flying blind. He'd hand over his documents to his accountant and hope for the best.

So we implemented a system. Nothing fancy. Just a weekly check-in where David would review his expenses and flag anything that might be tax-relevant. He'd log it in a simple spreadsheet and save the documentation.

And you know what happened? His anxiety disappeared. Not because he was suddenly saving thousands of dollars—his tax bill didn't change much—but because he felt like he understood what was going on. He felt like he had a handle on things.

That's the real power of this habit. It's not just about the money. It's about feeling competent and in control in an area of your life that often feels chaotic and overwhelming.

Now, I want to circle back to something I said earlier: the goal isn't perfection.

Because I think there's a tendency, especially among people who are already organized and conscientious, to overcomplicate this. To think that if they're going to track expenses, they need to do it *perfectly*. They need to categorize everything correctly, log every transaction, reconcile their records down to the penny.

And then, when that feels overwhelming, they don't do it at all.

Don't fall into that trap.

You're not trying to become a CPA. You're not trying to do your accountant's job. You're just trying to capture information so that when tax season comes, you have a starting point.

If you're not sure whether something is deductible, flag it anyway. You can sort it out later. If you forget to log a transaction one week, don't stress. Just add it the next week. If your categorization isn't perfect, that's fine. Your accountant can clean it up.

The system doesn't have to be perfect. It just has to exist.

Think about it like this: professional athletes don't just show up on game day and hope for the best. They spend hours practicing fundamental skills—shooting free throws, running drills, perfecting their technique. These aren't glamorous activities, but they're essential to success.

Similarly, managing your taxes isn't about finding some magical loophole that will save you thousands of dollars overnight. It's about consistently doing the small things—tracking expenses, documenting income, staying organized—that add up over time.

It's a long game. And it's a game you can win.

I had another client, Sarah, a graphic designer who ran her business out of her home office. She was meticulous about everything in her life—her design work, her fitness routine, even her grocery shopping list.

But when it came to taxes? Total chaos.

Every year she'd wait until the last minute, then spend days frantically gathering receipts and trying to reconstruct her expenses.

"I just hate dealing with money," she told me. "It stresses me out."

I asked her what specifically stressed her out. And she said it wasn't about the math. It was about not knowing where her money went. She felt like she was constantly losing track of things, and that made her anxious.

So we started with a simple system—a dedicated folder on her computer labeled "2024 Taxes." Every time she had an expense related to her business—software subscription, office supplies, even the portion of her internet bill allocated to her home office—she'd scan the receipt and save it in that folder.

It took her less than five minutes each time.

After a few weeks, something shifted. Sarah started looking forward to those little "tax check-ins." It wasn't about saving money. It was about feeling organized and in control. She felt like she had a handle on her finances, and that reduced her stress levels significantly.

And when tax season rolled around? It was shockingly easy. No more frantic searching. No more reconstructing months-old transactions. Just a clean folder with everything she needed.

The financial savings were nice—she claimed about $2,800 more in deductions than she had the previous year—but the real win was the peace of mind.

She told me later, "I didn't realize how much mental energy I was spending worrying about this until I stopped worrying about it."

And I think that's true for a lot of people. The anxiety of tax season isn't just about the money. It's about the feeling of being unprepared, of not knowing where your money went, of suspecting you left something on the table.

It's a low-grade stress that lingers for weeks, and it drains energy from everything else in your life.

So here's what I want you to do.

Not tomorrow. Not next week. Right now.

Take out your phone. Open your calendar. And set a recurring reminder for next Tuesday at 8 PM. (Or Wednesday. Or Friday. Or whatever day works for you.)

Label it "Tax check-in."

That's it. Just set the reminder.

Because here's the thing: you can read this entire chapter, nod along, think "Yeah, that makes sense," and then do absolutely nothing. And nothing will change.

Or you can take one small step. Right now. A tiny commitment to taking control.

What's the worst that could happen? Five minutes of your time?

And what's the best that could happen?

The possibility of reclaiming thousands of dollars. The peace of mind that comes from knowing you're not leaving money on the table. The sense of control that comes from engaging with the system instead of being passively swept along by it.

That's not a bad return on investment.

I think about this in terms of compound interest, which is something we'll talk about more in later chapters. But the principle applies here too.

Small actions, repeated consistently over time, compound into something much larger.

Tom didn't save $3,400 in one dramatic moment. He saved it seven minutes at a time, week after week, for an entire year.

Sarah didn't reclaim $2,800 by suddenly getting organized overnight. She did it five minutes at a time, receipt by receipt, transaction by transaction.

And the peace of mind they gained? That compounded too. Less anxiety in March. Less stress in April. More confidence in their ability to manage their finances going forward.

This is how you build a financial life that works *for* you instead of *against* you. Not through grand gestures or dramatic overhauls, but through small, sustainable habits that add up over time.

Because here's the uncomfortable truth: the system isn't going to change. The tax code isn't going to simplify. The IRS isn't going to start sending you helpful reminders about deductions you're missing.

The only thing you can control is how you engage with it.

You can keep doing what you've always done—scrambling in March, hoping you haven't forgotten anything, leaving money on the table—or you can build a habit that protects your money and gives you peace of mind.

The choice is yours.

But let me ask you this: what are you waiting for?

What's going to be different next year if you don't change something now?

You'll file your taxes. You'll get your refund or pay your bill. And you'll tell yourself, "Next year, I'm going to stay organized."

And next year will come, and you'll be right back where you started.

Unless you build a habit. Unless you take control. Unless you engage with the system instead of letting it happen to you.

So set the reminder. Start the habit. Protect your money.

And then, in Chapter 8, we'll talk about how to pull all of this together into a year-end checklist that ensures you're not leaving anything on the table when it's time to file.

Because here's what I've learned, both from my own experience and from watching hundreds of clients go through this: the hardest part isn't the tracking itself. It's not logging a receipt or updating a spreadsheet. The hardest part is believing that it matters before you see the results.

When you're standing in a parking lot with a crumpled receipt in your hand, it doesn't feel like you're building wealth. It feels like busy work. It feels like something a more organized person would do, not you.

But that's the lie your brain tells you to keep you comfortable.

Because if you convince yourself that tracking doesn't matter, then you don't have to feel bad about not doing it. You get to stay in the familiar pattern of scrambling at tax time, of wondering if you missed something, of hoping the IRS doesn't ask questions.

And sure, that pattern is stressful. But it's *known* stress. It's predictable. You survive it every year.

What's uncomfortable is stepping into a new pattern. What's uncomfortable is doing something today that won't pay off until April. What's uncomfortable is acting like someone who has their financial life together before you actually feel like that person.

But that's exactly how you become that person.

You don't wait until you feel organized to start organizing. You start organizing, and the feeling follows. You don't wait until you're confident about taxes to start tracking. You start tracking, and the confidence builds.

This is the gap that most people never cross. They wait for motivation that never comes. They wait to "feel ready." They wait for the perfect system, the perfect app, the perfect moment.

And while they're waiting, another year slips by.

So let me tell you what the habit actually looks like when it's working. Not the idealized version. Not the Instagram-perfect spreadsheet. The real thing.

It looks like taking a photo of a receipt while you're still standing at the register, because you know if you wait until you get home, you'll forget.

It looks like spending two minutes on a Sunday morning reviewing your transactions from the week, catching things before they pile up.

It looks like having a conversation with your spouse about a big purchase *before* you make it, not because you need permission, but because you're thinking about the tax implications together.

It looks like feeling a weird little surge of satisfaction when you file something correctly, because you've started to see the system as something you control instead of something that controls you.

It looks like making a mistake, missing a receipt, forgetting to log something—and then just catching it the next week instead of spiraling into shame and giving up entirely.

Because here's the other thing nobody tells you about building this habit: you're going to mess up. You're going to have a week where you don't log anything. You're going to lose a receipt. You're going to forget to track mileage for a trip.

And when that happens, your brain is going to try to convince you that the whole system is broken, that you're not cut out for this, that you should just go back to the old way.

Don't listen.

One missed week doesn't erase the three weeks you did track. One lost receipt doesn't invalidate the twenty you saved. One forgotten trip doesn't mean you should stop logging mileage altogether.

You just start again. You pick up where you left off. You keep going.

This is what separates people who build the habit from people who try and quit. The people who succeed aren't more disciplined. They're not more naturally organized. They just don't treat a single failure as proof that the whole thing doesn't work.

They treat it as part of the process.

And the process works. Not perfectly. Not elegantly. But it works.

I've seen people go from shoebox chaos to having their entire year organized in a single folder. I've seen people cut their tax prep time in half. I've seen people find deductions they didn't even know existed, just because they were actually looking at their expenses throughout the year instead of trying to reconstruct everything in March.

But more than that, I've seen people stop being afraid of their taxes.

That's the real shift. That's what makes this worth doing.

Because when you're engaged with the system, when you're tracking throughout the year, when you know what's coming—taxes stop being this scary, mysterious thing that happens to you. They become something you manage. Something you understand. Something you control.

And that shift changes everything.

It changes how you make financial decisions. It changes how you think about your business or your investments. It changes how you feel in January when everyone else is panicking and you're just calmly reviewing numbers you've already seen.

It gives you power.

Not power over the IRS. Not power to cheat the system or dodge your obligations.

Power over yourself. Over your choices. Over your financial future.

And that power comes from a habit that starts with a single logged receipt. A single tracked mile. A single moment where you chose to engage instead of ignore.

So if you take nothing else from this chapter, take this: start smaller than you think you need to. Start so small it feels almost silly.

One receipt a week. One mileage log a month. One quarterly check-in.

Just start.

Because the habit you build in August will save you in April. The system you set up today will protect you tomorrow. The choice you make right now will compound over time into something that actually changes your relationship with money.

And when tax season rolls around next year, you won't be the person scrambling to piece together a year's worth of chaos.

You'll be the person who's ready.

The tracker told Rick everything he'd spent in 2025. It couldn't tell him what he should do about it before the year closed.

Chapter 8: Putting It All Together: A Year-End Tax Checklist

Rick's refund check was $3,400. Not a round number, not a clean windfall, just the specific arithmetic of his withholding minus his liability. It sat on his desk for a week, not because he didn't know what to do with it, but because he was trying to reverse-engineer what it meant.

When I looked at my own refund check that December, I didn't prop it up anywhere. I pulled out my W-4 and calculated how much I'd overpaid per month—$283—and opened my spreadsheet to see what I could have done with it.

When Rick stared at his refund check, he saw what Maria had seen a year earlier: not a windfall, but a loan he'd made without asking, finally returned.

I remember staring at that refund check on my desk, suddenly seeing it not as a windfall but as proof of a system designed for one thing: maximum collection, minimal tolerance. Every deduction, every credit, every loophole wasn't some benevolent gift from Uncle Sam; it was the result of hard-fought battles waged by people who understood exactly how the game was played. And if you weren't actively playing – organizing receipts, tracking expenses, knowing what you were entitled to—you were essentially surrendering.

Most people do surrender, quietly and consistently. They treat taxes like a weather event: unavoidable, unpleasant, something that happens *to* them, not something they participate in. Come March and April, it's a frantic scramble for forgotten forms, guesstimates on charitable donations, and a desperate hope that whatever number the software spits out is reasonably accurate. Then comes the promise—always broken—of doing better next year.

It's a familiar cycle, and it reminds me of trying to eat healthier without changing what's in your fridge. You might manage a week or two fueled by willpower, but eventually, you revert to the path of least resistance: pre-packaged meals and late-night takeout. Similarly, "doing better" with taxes requires more than good intentions; it demands a system, a proactive approach that extends beyond those frantic few weeks before the deadline.

Think about Sarah Chen, a graphic designer I worked with on a project last year. She's meticulous—almost obsessively so—about everything in her life, from color palettes to font choices. Except taxes. Every April, she'd hand over a chaotic mess of receipts and bank statements to her accountant, bracing herself for a hefty bill and the inevitable feeling of being ripped off. This wasn't about laziness; it was about lacking a framework, a way to translate her natural organizational skills into something applicable to tax season. She had the capacity to be proactive, she just didn't know *how*.

The fix isn't becoming a CPA—that's neither necessary nor desirable for most people. It's building a simple, repeatable year-end checklist, not as a last-minute fire drill but as the culmination of consistent effort throughout the year. It shifts your mindset from reactive to proactive, transforming tax season from a source of dread into an exercise in confirmation and control.

Let's start with something seemingly mundane: Form W-4. The one you filled out when you started your current job. I'll bet money you haven't touched it since. Maybe six months ago? Six years? Regardless, the IRS is still withholding taxes based on a version of your life that likely no longer exists. Life changes—marriage, divorce, kids, a new house, a side hustle—all impact your tax picture.

Your withholding should adapt accordingly. But it won't unless you intervene.

And here's the kicker: if you don't update your W-4, you're either overpaying all year (leaving money on the table) or underpaying (facing penalties and interest). Neither scenario is ideal. It feels strange to actively *reduce* your withholding when you're used to thinking of a refund as a win, but that's precisely the point. A large refund isn't free money; it's an indication that you've been overpaying throughout the year. Think of it this way: would you willingly loan someone interest-free for twelve months? Of course not. Yet, that's exactly what most people do with the IRS.

I remember a conversation I had with my friend David—a carpenter who'd recently started a woodworking business on the side. He was ecstatic about his $800 refund, bragging about how he was going to use it for a weekend getaway. I gently pointed out that $800 was effectively eight months of free labor he'd given the government, money he could have reinvested in tools or marketing for his new business. He hadn't thought of it that way before. He saw the refund as a reward; I tried to explain it as an opportunity cost.

Updating your W-4 isn't complicated. The IRS has a free online estimator—Tax Withholding Estimator—that walks you through the process step by step. It takes about twenty minutes, but those twenty minutes could easily translate into hundreds of dollars in savings over the year. Set a reminder for late November, before the December chaos sets in, and get it done.

Next up: expenses. This is where people either become paralyzed with overwhelm or dangerously overconfident. The overwhelmed assume it's too complicated and give up entirely. The overconfident believe they'll remember everything without documentation. Both groups lose money.

If you're self-employed, or if you have side income reported on a Schedule C, tracking expenses is non-negotiable. Not just the big ones—laptop, software subscriptions, office space—but the small, easily forgotten items that add up over time: that online course in March, the domain renewal in July, the coffee shop receipt from a client meeting in October. Individually, they seem insignificant. Collectively, they can represent hundreds—even thousands—of dollars in deductible expenses.

The IRS doesn't care *how* you track them—spreadsheet, folder, shoebox—as long as you do. What doesn't work is relying on memory. Take the case of Emily Carter, a freelance writer I consulted with last year. She was diligent about tracking her income but completely neglected expenses. She remembered the big purchases—her laptop, her monitor—but had no record of the smaller ones: Grammarly subscriptions, online courses, even mileage for client meetings. At tax time, she estimated her total deductible expenses at around $500. A quick review of her bank statements revealed a figure closer to $1200. She'd left over $700 on the table—money she was legally entitled to claim.

Your year-end checklist is your safety net for catching these missed opportunities. In early December, sit down with your bank and credit card statements and meticulously review each transaction. Flag anything that might be deductible or credit-eligible. If you're unsure whether something qualifies, err on the side of caution and ask your tax preparer. It's better to over-document than under-document.

And while you're at it, double-check your categorization. Did you accidentally lump home office expenses with general office supplies? Did you forget to separate the business portion of your internet bill?

These aren't gotchas; they're simply details that matter. December is your opportunity to fix them before they become problems.

Finally, let's talk about credits. A deduction reduces your taxable income—the amount subject to tax. A credit, on the other hand, directly reduces your actual tax bill, dollar for dollar. That makes credits far more valuable than deductions and also easier to overlook.

The Child Tax Credit is probably the most well-known, but there are many others: The Earned Income Tax Credit (often overlooked), the American Opportunity Tax Credit for college expenses, credits for energy-efficient home improvements, even credits for adopting a child or contributing to a retirement account. The IRS has a comprehensive list on their website—it's long, but worth browsing.

Don't assume you don't qualify just because you haven't claimed a credit before. It's easy to fall into the trap of thinking these benefits are for "other people"—those with kids, those in school, those who own homes. But the range is surprisingly broad, and the only way to know for sure is to check.

The year-end checklist isn't simply a list of tasks to complete; it's the capstone of a system you should be building all year long. It's about turning taxes from an annual headache into an ongoing process—categorizing expenses as they happen, scanning receipts and saving them in a dedicated folder, flagging potential deductions or credits throughout the year. This groundwork transforms December from a frantic scramble for information into a focused review of what you already know.

Let me give you a system you can actually use. I call it the Year-Round Tax Tracker, and it's built around the idea that taxes aren't something you *do* once a year; they're an ongoing conversation with your income. It's about shifting from damage control in April to proactive management all year long. And the best part? It doesn't require becoming a tax savant or spending hours poring over IRS publications. Just consistent, small actions that add up to big savings.

Start with a dedicated folder – digital is fine, physical if you prefer the tactile feel of paper. The key is consistency. This isn't about perfect organization from day one; it's about creating a single place where tax-relevant information accumulates throughout the year. Think of it as your financial early warning system. A receipt for that home office chair? In the folder. A statement showing charitable donations? In the folder. The confirmation email from that online course you took to improve your skills? You guessed it – in the folder.

Don't wait until December to start. That's like deciding to get in shape on January 1st after a month of holiday cookies. It feels overwhelming, and the odds of success are low. Instead, make it part of your routine. Whenever you receive a document that *might* be tax-deductible or credit-eligible, file it immediately. I used to leave things piled up on my desk for weeks, telling myself I'd get to it "later." Later never came. Now, as soon as something crosses my path—a receipt, a statement, an invoice—I scan it (or file the paper copy) and move on. It takes seconds, and it prevents that December panic.

Next, embrace the power of categorization. Your folder doesn't need to be meticulously organized into subfolders labeled "Medical Expenses," "Charitable Donations," and "Business Deductions" right away. Start broad—just separate business from personal if you're self-employed or have side income. But as you accumulate documents, start adding tags or labels. This makes it infinitely easier to find what you need when tax season rolls around. Most cloud storage services allow tagging; even a simple naming convention like

"Business - Office Supplies - 2024" can save you hours of searching later.

Don't underestimate the value of regular reconciliation. Once a month, take fifteen minutes to review your bank and credit card statements. Look for anything that might be deductible or credit-eligible. Did you buy books related to your profession? Pay for professional development courses? Donate to charity? Flag those transactions—either in your digital folder with tags or by highlighting them on the physical statements. This isn't about obsessively tracking every penny; it's about creating a running list of potential deductions so nothing slips through the cracks.

Now, let's talk about specific expenses. If you're an employee, keep track of unreimbursed business expenses—things like professional dues, work-related travel, or home office supplies (if you qualify). Even if you don't itemize your deductions, these can sometimes be claimed as adjustments to income. For self-employed individuals, the options are even wider: advertising costs, insurance premiums, legal fees, and a whole host of other expenses that can reduce your taxable income. The IRS website has detailed guidance on what's deductible, but when in doubt, err on the side of documenting it.

And don't forget about those often-overlooked credits. The Lifetime Learning Credit can help cover tuition costs for courses taken to improve your job skills—even if you're not pursuing a formal degree. The Child and Dependent Care Credit can offset expenses related to childcare while you work or look for work. And the Energy Efficient Home Improvement Credit can provide tax breaks for making energy-saving upgrades to your home. These credits aren't automatic; you have to actively claim them, which means knowing they exist and gathering the necessary documentation.

The checklist itself—the thing we're building towards—isn't about discovering new deductions in December. It's about *confirming* that you've already captured everything you're entitled to. Think of it as a final audit of your tax year. Start with your W-2 and 1099 forms, making sure they match the income reported on your spreadsheet or accounting software. Then, review your expense folder, checking off each category—business expenses, medical expenses, charitable donations, etc.—and ensuring you have sufficient documentation to support your claims.

I remember a client I worked with a few years ago, Sarah, who was a freelance writer like me. She'd been tracking her expenses diligently all year, but she still felt anxious as tax season approached. She worried that she'd missed something—a deduction here, a credit there. So we sat down together in December and went through her checklist, one item at a time. As we reviewed each category, she realized that she'd actually captured more deductions than she thought. The process wasn't stressful; it was reassuring. She felt confident that she was maximizing her tax savings without taking any unnecessary risks.

That's the goal. Not to find loopholes or exploit the system. But to engage with it—to understand your rights and responsibilities as a taxpayer, and to claim every deduction and credit you're legally entitled to. It's about leveling the playing field. Because let's be honest: the tax code is complex, and it favors those who know how to navigate it.

Don't fall into the trap of thinking this is only for high-income earners or business owners. Every taxpayer—regardless of income level—can benefit from proactive tax planning. Even small deductions can add up over time, and every dollar saved is a dollar you can put towards your goals: paying off debt, saving for retirement, investing in your future.

So here's the challenge: this week, create that dedicated folder. Start categorizing your expenses. And commit to spending just fifteen minutes a month reviewing your bank statements. It's not glamorous work, but it's powerful. It transforms taxes from an annual headache into an ongoing process—a system you build and refine over time.

Because here's the thing about systems: they don't require willpower. They require setup. Once the habits are in place, the work becomes automatic. And that frees you up to focus on what really matters—living your life, pursuing your passions, and building a future you're excited about.

And it leaves you with a question, not an answer: What could *you* do with an extra $50 a month? An extra $200? An extra $1,000? The tax code is full of possibilities, but only if you're willing to look for them.

…You're going to spend the time one way or another. You can spend it in December, when you have breathing room and nothing's on fire, reviewing records you've been keeping all year and making small adjustments. Or you can spend it in April, when the deadline's looming and your stress level's through the roof, trying to reconstruct an entire year's worth of financial activity from memory and random receipts stuffed in a drawer. One of those experiences is manageable. The other is miserable. And the miserable version costs you money. Not just in missed deductions—though that's real—but in preparer fees. If you walk into a CPA's office in March with a shoebox full of unsorted receipts and a vague sense of what you earned, they're going to charge you a premium to sort through the chaos. If you walk in with an organized spreadsheet, clear documentation, and all your forms already gathered, the bill's going to be a lot lower. Because you're not paying them to do detective work. You're paying them to prepare your return, which is what they're actually good at. So yeah, the year-end checklist is work. But it's work that pays you back—in lower stress, lower fees, and higher certainty that you're keeping as much of what you earned as you legally can.

Let me give you a system you can actually use. I call it the Year-Round Tax Tracker, and it's built around the idea that taxes aren't an annual event—they're an ongoing process. It's not about finding hidden loopholes or trying to beat the IRS. It's about knowing what you're entitled to claim and making sure you don't leave any money on the table. The first step is simple: a dedicated folder, digital or physical. Doesn't matter which, as long as it becomes your tax headquarters. Think of it as mission control for your finances. Everything related to taxes—receipts, statements, forms, notes—goes in that folder. No exceptions.

I used to be a minimalist about this, thinking I could just scan everything and toss the paper. But I learned the hard way that there's something reassuring about having the physical receipt as backup, especially when dealing with bigger expenses or potential audits. So now I do both: scan it for quick access and file the original in my folder. It adds a little bit of clutter, but it saves me a lot of headaches.

Next comes categorization. This is where most people get bogged down, trying to be too precise. Forget about creating dozens of subcategories with intricate labels. Keep it simple. Four buckets are enough: Income, Business Expenses (if applicable), Medical Expenses, and Charitable Donations. Everything else can fall into one of those four categories. If you're self-employed or have side income, add a fifth category for estimated tax payments.

The key is consistency. Every time you receive a statement, invoice, or receipt, file it immediately in the appropriate folder. Don't let things pile up. The longer you wait, the harder it becomes to reconstruct what happened and the more likely you are to forget something important. And don't just toss it in haphazardly. Take thirty seconds to jot down a brief description on the receipt or statement—what it was for, when you paid it, who you paid it to. Future-you will thank you for that little bit of effort.

Now, let's talk about tracking. A spreadsheet is fine, but I prefer a dedicated app. There are dozens out there, some free, some subscription-based. Find one that suits your needs and learn how to use it. The beauty of an app is that it can automate a lot of the work—categorizing expenses, generating reports, even reminding you to scan receipts. But don't rely on the app completely. Always double-check its work. Apps make mistakes, just like people do.

And here's where I get a little obsessive: monthly reconciliation. At the end of every month, I sit down with my bank statements and credit card statements and compare them to my records. It takes maybe an hour, but it's worth it. It catches errors early—duplicate entries, incorrect categories, missed expenses—before they become major problems. And it gives me a sense of control over my finances. I know exactly where my money is going, and I know that my tax records are accurate and up-to-date.

I remember one year discovering a $400 charge on my credit card for something I hadn't authorized—a subscription to some obscure streaming service I never signed up for. If I hadn't been reconciling my statements every month, it would have taken months to discover the fraud. And who knows how much more they would have charged me by then?

That monthly check-in isn't just about catching errors, though. It's also about identifying potential deductions and credits you might be missing. Did you donate to a charity this month? Did you pay for medical expenses out of pocket? Did you incur any business expenses that haven't been reimbursed? If so, make sure they're properly documented and categorized.

And finally, the year-end checklist itself. This is where everything comes together. In early December—before the holiday madness sets in—pull out your tax folder and review all your records for the entire year. Start with your W-2s and 1099s. Make sure you've received them from all your employers and clients. If not, contact them immediately.

Next, go through each of your expense categories and verify that everything is accurate and complete. Double-check your totals, confirm that you have supporting documentation for every deduction or credit you plan to claim, and identify any areas where you might need additional information.

Then move on to the tax forms themselves. The IRS website has instructions for all the most common forms—Schedule A (Itemized Deductions), Schedule C (Profit or Loss From Business), Form 1040-EZ (Income Tax Return for Single and Joint Filers), etc. Download them, read the instructions carefully, and fill them out as much as possible before you hand them over to your tax preparer.

Look, I'm not a CPA. I don't pretend to be. But I know enough about taxes to recognize when something doesn't feel right. And that gut feeling has saved me thousands of dollars over the years. If you're unsure about anything—a deduction you might qualify for, a rule you don't understand, a form you can't decipher—don't hesitate to ask for help. A good tax preparer is worth their weight in gold.

I've seen too many people fall into the trap of thinking they can save money by doing their taxes themselves, only to end up making costly mistakes or missing out on valuable deductions. It's like trying to fix your own car when you have no mechanical experience. You might get lucky, but you're more likely to make things worse.

The point isn't about eliminating taxes—that's not realistic. The point is about minimizing them legally and ethically. About knowing what you're entitled to claim and making sure you don't leave any money on the table. It's about taking control of your finances and building a system that works for you, year after year.

Think of it this way: taxes aren't just an annual obligation; they're a reflection of your financial life. They tell a story about how you earned your money, how you spent it, and how you invested it. And if you pay attention to that story, you can learn a lot about yourself—your priorities, your habits, your strengths and weaknesses.

So take the time to build a Year-Round Tax Tracker. It's not glamorous work, but it's powerful. It transforms taxes from an annual headache into an ongoing process—a system you build and refine over time. Because here's the thing about systems: they don't require willpower. They require setup. Once the habits are in place, the work becomes automatic. And that frees you up to focus on what really matters—living your life, pursuing your passions, and building a future you're excited about.

And it leaves you with a question, not an answer: What if, instead of bracing for April 15th every year, you woke up knowing exactly where you stood? Not just financially, but in terms of proactively shaping your tax outcome *throughout* the year? What could that peace of mind be worth?

When Rick stared at his refund check, he saw what Maria had seen a year earlier: not a windfall, but a loan he'd made without asking, finally returned. The checklist had shown him what he'd missed. The system would show him how to stop missing it.

Rick knew what to do in December. The question was: would he remember in January?

Chapter 9: The Proactive Taxpayer System: From Reactive to Planned

I still remember the exact moment I understood the difference between knowing what I should do and actually having a system that made me do it. It wasn't at my kitchen table in March, surrounded by shoeboxes—though I've been there, more times than I'd like to admit. It was in December.

When the IRS letter arrived the following October—same envelope, same Thursday—I opened it immediately. I knew exactly what it would say. I'd planned for it.

It wasn't at my kitchen table in March, surrounded by shoeboxes—though I've been there, more times than I'd like to admit. It was in December. A Tuesday. I was sitting in my accountant's office for what I'd thought would be a quick year-end check-in, and she slid a single piece of paper across the desk with a number on it. My projected tax liability for the year.

The number was fine. Expected, even. What wasn't fine was the follow-up question: "So what do you want to do about it?"

I just stared at her. What did I want to *do* about it? It was December. The year was essentially over. What could I possibly do?

Turns out: quite a lot. We spent the next forty-five minutes running scenarios. If I maxed out my retirement contribution before December 31st, the number dropped by $3,200. If I prepaid my January mortgage payment, I could pull that deduction into the current year since I was itemizing anyway—another $800. If I made the charitable donation I'd been planning to make in January during the holidays instead, that was $500 more. We kept finding levers.

Small adjustments, most of them things I was going to do anyway, just shifted by a few weeks. By the time we finished, we'd knocked almost $5,000 off my tax bill.

I walked out of that office feeling two things simultaneously: relief that I'd just saved five grand, and absolute fury at myself for not knowing any of this before December. How much had I left on the table in previous years? How many opportunities had closed on December 31st while I was busy with the holidays, blissfully unaware that the tax clock was ticking?

The tax code isn't designed to minimize what you owe. It's designed to collect the maximum you'll tolerate without pushing back. Every deduction, every credit, every adjustment exists because someone fought for it. And if you don't claim it, the IRS certainly won't remind you. This isn't adversarial; it's structural. You have to engage, or you lose by default.

Most people know this intellectually. But there's a gap—sometimes a canyon—between knowing you should plan ahead and actually doing it.

My neighbor Chris is sitting at his kitchen table right now. I can see him through my window. It's March 23rd, and he's surrounded by what looks like the aftermath of a paper explosion. Shoeboxes, grocery bags, a stack of envelopes still sealed from last summer. I recognize that particular kind of panic in his eyes because I wore it myself for years—the panic that comes from realizing you have three weeks to reconstruct an entire year of financial activity from memory and chaos.

Chris keeps saying, "I know I had those receipts. I *know* I had them."

He did. Probably. The project management course from June that cost him $1,400. The certification exam in October, another $600. Both qualified professional development expenses. Both fully deductible. Both lost somewhere in that avalanche of paper that's been migrating from his car trunk to his junk drawer to the top of his refrigerator for the past twelve months.

But here's what bothers me more than the money Chris is leaving on the table. It's the way this annual ritual erodes your sense of control. You start each year thinking you'll do better this time. You'll save receipts. You'll track expenses. You'll stay organized. And then February rolls into March, March slides into early April, and suddenly you're back at that table with the shoeboxes. The main feeling isn't even frustration anymore—it's resignation. This is just how it is. This is just how it works. The system is too complicated, you're too busy, and the best you can hope for is to survive tax season without penalties.

That resignation is the real cost. Because once you accept that tax season is something that happens *to* you rather than something you control, you've already surrendered. Not just this year's deductions, but next year's too. And the year after that. You've given up the only real leverage you have.

Let me show you exactly what that surrender costs.

Say you do everything right in March. You gather every document, categorize every expense, claim every deduction you're entitled to. You file on time. You might even get a refund. Success, right?

Not exactly. Because what you're doing is optimizing *last year's* situation based on decisions you made months ago without full information. You're flying blind for eleven months and then trying to course-correct in the twelfth. And the most effective tax strategies—the ones that actually move the needle—require action *during* the year, not after it's over.

Take retirement contributions. If you're self-employed, you can contribute to a SEP IRA and reduce your taxable income significantly. The amount you're allowed to contribute is based on your net self-employment income, which you won't know with certainty until the year is over. If you wait until March to think about it, you've lost the opportunity to make strategic contributions throughout the year based on how your income is actually trending. You might scramble to max out your contribution in early April—technically you have until the filing deadline—but you've missed months of potential tax-advantaged growth. More importantly, you've lost the ability to adjust your estimated tax payments throughout the year to reflect those contributions, which means you might overpay quarterly taxes and essentially give the government an interest-free loan. Again.

Or consider tax-loss harvesting. If you have investments that have declined in value, you can sell them to realize the loss and offset capital gains—or even offset up to $3,000 of ordinary income. But this only works if you identify the opportunity while the loss exists and before December 31st. If you're not monitoring your portfolio with tax implications in mind throughout the year, you'll miss it. By the time you're thinking about taxes in March, the market may have recovered. The opportunity isn't just harder to capture. It's *gone*. The door closed on December 31st, and you weren't paying attention because December is the holidays, not tax season.

I need you to sit with that for a second. There are tax strategies that expire. They have deadlines built into them that have nothing to do with when you file your return. You can have a perfect March and still lose, because the game was already over before you showed up.

You're probably thinking this sounds like a lot of work. I'm barely keeping up as it is. I just want to file my taxes and move on.

I get it. I really do. But here's what I've learned after years of doing this both the reactive way and the proactive way: a small amount of consistent effort throughout the year—thirty minutes a month, maybe an hour during busier periods—will save you significantly more time and money than the annual scramble. More than that, it will eliminate that low-grade anxiety that starts around February and doesn't lift until you hit "submit" on the return in mid-April. You know the one. That constant background hum of *I should be doing something but I'm not sure what* that follows you around like elevator music for your stress response.

The tool that makes this possible is what I call the Tax Planning Calendar, though calling it a "calendar" almost undersells it. Think of it less like another obligation on your schedule and more like scheduled maintenance for your finances. You don't wait until your car is smoking on the side of the road to check the oil. You do it regularly, on a schedule, because it prevents bigger problems and costs a fraction of what you'd pay if you ignored it until something broke.

Same principle here. You're not trying to become a tax professional. You're not spending hours every week obsessing over IRS publications. You're building awareness and documentation incrementally, so that by the time December rolls around, you're not starting from zero. You're not even starting from fifty. You're at ninety, just tightening bolts.

Here's the framework. Each month has a focus—a specific task or area of attention that takes thirty to sixty minutes. Some months less, if nothing much is happening. Some months slightly more, if you hit a busy period or a major life change. But the workload is distributed across twelve months instead of compressed into three panicked weeks in March.

January is document gathering. Not filing. Not categorizing. Just collecting. W-2s, 1099s, any income statements. You're creating a central file—physical or digital, doesn't matter—where everything tax-related lives. The goal is to have one place you can go when you need something, not seventeen shoeboxes scattered across your house. I use a physical folder labeled with the year because I'm old-fashioned that way and I like being able to toss paper into something without firing up my laptop. You might prefer Dropbox or Google Drive. The medium matters less than the commitment: one place, everything goes there, no exceptions.

The first year I did this, I cheated. I put the folder on my kitchen counter where I'd see it every single day, and I made a deal with myself: any time I walked past it with something in my hand that might possibly be tax-relevant, I'd toss it in. Bank statement? Toss. Receipt for the freelance software I expense? Toss. That 1099 from the consulting gig? Toss. No thinking, no organizing, just collecting. By the end of January I had a folder about two inches thick. Took me maybe five cumulative minutes of actual effort, because I'd designed the system to require zero willpower.

February is expense categorization. Take the receipts and statements you've accumulated and start sorting them into broad categories. Business expenses if you're self-employed. Charitable donations. Medical bills. Nothing fancy. You're not preparing a tax return; you're organizing raw data so it's usable later. I use a simple spreadsheet with columns for date, vendor, amount, and category. Takes me maybe forty-five minutes. Sometimes less if January was slow.

March is last year's return review. Pull out your previous year's tax return and actually look at it. Not for the refund amount—though sure, that's nice—but for patterns. Did you miss any deductions? Were there credits you didn't claim? Did your income change significantly? This isn't self-flagellation. It's data gathering. You're looking for insights that can inform this year's strategy.

The first time I did this, I realized I'd been eligible for the self-employment health insurance deduction for *three years* and never claimed it because I didn't know it existed. That one line was worth over a thousand dollars a year. Three years. I'd left three thousand dollars on the table out of pure ignorance—not because the IRS hid it from me, but because I'd never looked closely enough at my own return to notice the gap.

April is life changes check-in. Did anything significant happen in the past few months? New job, marriage, baby, home purchase, side hustle? These events impact your tax situation, and if you don't adjust your W-4 withholding accordingly, you're either overpaying all year—free loan to the government—or underpaying and setting yourself up for penalties. The IRS has a W-4 estimator tool online. It's not perfect, but it's decent. And it's free. Use it.

May through August are the quiet months. You're not doing heavy lifting—just maintaining your system. As receipts come in, file them. As expenses occur, note them. If you anticipate a big change in income or deductions, this is when you consider mid-year withholding adjustments. The key is consistency, not intensity. I spend maybe fifteen minutes a month during these stretches. Sometimes I skip a month entirely if nothing much happened. The world doesn't end.

September is when it starts getting interesting. You've got three months left in the year. Based on what's happened so far, what does your full-year income look like? What deductions can you reasonably expect to claim? You're not filing anything yet—you're building a rough estimate so you can identify gaps or opportunities. For the first time, you're not just documenting what happened. You're projecting what's coming and realizing you still have time to influence it.

October is scenario planning. This is where the calendar stops being a documentation tool and becomes a strategy tool. What if you max out your retirement contributions? What if you itemize instead of taking the standard deduction? What if you prepay some January expenses in December to pull the deduction into the current year? You're running "what if" scenarios to see which strategies might work in your favor. Some won't pencil out. Some will. You won't know until you model it. And the only way to model it is to have data—the data you've been collecting all year.

I know this sounds abstract. Let me show you what it looks like in practice.

Maria is a freelance graphic designer. Her income fluctuates. Some months she's slammed with client work and pulling late nights; other months she's pitching proposals and hoping something lands. For years, tax season was her annual nightmare. Last year she decided enough was enough. Not because she'd suddenly become more disciplined—Maria would be the first to tell you she's neither organized nor particularly good with money—but because she was tired of the panic. Tired of feeling like she was leaving money on the table but unable to prove it.

In January, she gathered her 1099-NEC forms from clients. Didn't try to categorize anything. Just collection. A folder on her desktop labeled "Taxes 2027" became the home for everything potentially relevant. Bank statements, invoices, receipt images from her phone. All in one place. Total time investment: maybe twenty minutes.

February: one hour sorting receipts into categories. Software subscriptions for her design tools—Adobe Creative Cloud, Figma, a couple of smaller apps she used for mockups. Home office expenses—a portion of her rent, utilities, internet. Mileage for the handful of in-person client meetings she'd had. Professional development—that online course on brand identity she took in June because she was trying to expand into logo work. Still rough. Still not tax-return-ready. But organized enough to be useful.

March: she pulled out last year's return, and one line jumped out at her. Self-employment health insurance deduction. She'd qualified for it but didn't claim it because she didn't realize it existed. That single missed deduction cost her over a thousand dollars. She made a note—on paper, taped to her monitor where she'd see it every day—to claim it this year.

April brought a curveball. A new client came through with a long-term contract. Six months, significant retainer, way more stable income than Maria was used to. She was thrilled. She was also nervous, because this was going to push her income up by about 30% over what she'd made the previous year. She immediately recalculated her estimated quarterly tax payments using a free online calculator. If she'd waited until the end of the year to realize her income had jumped, she would have underpaid her estimated taxes and faced penalties. A thirty-minute adjustment in April saved her hundreds.

May through August were quiet. She added receipts to her folder as they came in, spent maybe fifteen minutes a month keeping her expense tracker current. Nothing heroic. Just maintenance. One month she forgot entirely and had to catch up the next month. Took an extra ten minutes. No disaster.

September: she projected her year-end income using data from previous years and her current contracts. It looked like she'd come in about 20% higher than last year—good for business, but it meant her tax liability would increase too. She ran a rough estimate using TurboTax's free calculator and identified a gap between what she'd paid in quarterly taxes so far and what she'd likely owe. Not huge, but significant enough that she needed to adjust her Q4 payment up.

October was when the calendar really paid off. She played with scenarios. What if she maxed out a SEP IRA contribution? She ran the numbers. A $10,000 contribution would reduce her taxable income by $10,000, saving her roughly $2,500 in federal taxes at her marginal rate, plus another chunk in self-employment taxes—call it $3,000 total. The retirement contribution was money she was planning to save anyway. This just made it tax-advantaged. She also looked at whether itemizing made sense this year. It didn't quite pencil out; the standard deduction was still higher. But it was close enough that she made a note to track charitable donations more carefully next year.

November is finalization. Lock in your decisions from October. If you're increasing your retirement contribution, set it up. If you're making a charitable donation before year-end, schedule it. Gather documentation for any major deductions you plan to claim. Run a preliminary tax estimate using software or a calculator to see where you stand. By Thanksgiving, you should know—within a couple hundred dollars—what your tax liability will be. No surprises.

No panic.

Maria set up her SEP IRA contribution through her bank in mid-November. Gathered documentation for her home office deduction—lease, utility bills, a diagram showing the square footage of her workspace versus her total apartment. Ran a preliminary estimate using TurboTax to confirm she was on track. She was. Almost exactly.

December is final review. Double-check everything. Make sure you haven't missed any last-minute opportunities. If you're close to a deductible expense threshold—like medical expenses that have to exceed a percentage of your adjusted gross income—consider whether it makes sense to accelerate any planned expenses into December. Then close out the year with confidence, knowing you've done what you can.

Maria made one last charitable donation in December—something she would have done anyway, but timing it before year-end meant the deduction applied to the current year. When January rolled around, she wasn't starting from zero. She was handing her tax preparer a complete, organized file, and the preparer's only reaction was, "I wish all my clients did this."

Maria wasn't aiming for perfection. She just wanted to avoid the panic. But the side effect of building a system was optimization. When you're aware of your tax situation throughout the year, you naturally start making better decisions—not because you're a tax expert, but because you have the information you need when it matters.

Now, I know some of you are thinking, *I'm not self-employed. I just get a W-2. This doesn't really apply to me.*

Hold on. The mechanics are different, but the principle is the same. If you're a W-2 employee, you're not making quarterly estimated payments, but you *are* controlling your withholding through your W-4. And most people set their W-4 once—when they start a job—and never touch it again, even as their life circumstances change dramatically.

You get married. You have a kid. You buy a house and suddenly have a mortgage interest deduction big enough to make itemizing worthwhile. Each of these events should trigger a W-4 review, because your tax situation has fundamentally changed. But if you're only thinking about taxes in March, you miss the window to adjust. You end up either overpaying all year—giving the IRS an interest-free loan—or underpaying and facing a surprise bill in April.

Let's say you get married in June. Congratulations. Your tax situation just shifted, because now you're filing jointly and your combined income might push you into a different bracket. If you don't adjust your W-4, you're having taxes withheld based on your single filing status and your individual income. Come April, you might owe. Not because you did anything wrong, but because your withholding didn't keep pace with your actual tax liability.

Or say you have a baby in March. (Also congratulations.) You now qualify for the Child Tax Credit, which is worth a couple thousand dollars. That's money you don't owe. But if you don't adjust your W-4 to account for it, you're *still* having taxes withheld as if you didn't have the credit. You'll get the money back as a refund, sure. But in the meantime, you've been overpaying all year. You just gave the government an interest-free loan for nine months because you didn't update a form.

The calendar works for W-2 employees too. The tasks shift slightly—you're not tracking business expenses or making estimated payments—but the core principle remains: small, consistent attention throughout the year beats a panicked scramble in March.

January: Gather W-2s and any 1099s for side income or investment earnings. Create your central file.

February: Review last year's return. Did you miss anything? Were there credits or deductions you qualified for but didn't claim?

March: Life changes check-in. Marriage, baby, home purchase, new job? Adjust your W-4.

April through August: Monitor. If your income changes significantly—promotion, bonus, spouse starts or stops working—revisit your W-4.

September: Project your year-end income and deductions. Are you on track? Will you owe or get a refund?

October: Scenario planning. Should you increase your 401(k) contribution to reduce taxable income? Bunch charitable donations into one year to exceed the standard deduction threshold?

November: Finalize. Make any contributions, donations, or adjustments before year-end.

December: Final review. You should know, within a couple hundred bucks, what your tax situation looks like.

Does this guarantee you'll never owe? No. But it guarantees you won't be *surprised*. And surprise is where most financial pain lives.

Here's what I want you to understand: the tax system rewards attention. It doesn't reward expertise—you don't need to be a CPA to do this. It doesn't reward complexity—the strategies I'm describing are straightforward. It rewards *awareness*. Knowing your situation. Tracking your opportunities. Acting when the window is still open instead of discovering it closed three months after the fact.

The gap between reactive and proactive isn't knowledge. It's not even discipline, not really. It's having a system that makes the proactive choice feel easier than the reactive one. Right now, the reactive choice feels easier because it requires nothing from you for eleven months. The proactive choice feels harder because you're doing something consistently, even when it doesn't feel urgent.

But flip that. Build a system where documenting an expense takes fifteen seconds because you've already set up the folder and the spreadsheet. Where reviewing your tax situation takes thirty minutes in September because you've been tracking all year and the data is already organized. Where December is a confirmation step instead of a frantic scramble.

Once the system exists, the proactive choice becomes easier. And once it's easier, you'll actually do it. Not because you're more disciplined or motivated, but because the path of least resistance now leads toward the outcome you want instead of away from it.

That's what the Tax Planning Calendar does. It makes the invisible visible. It turns vague anxiety about taxes into concrete, manageable tasks. It gives you a roadmap so you're never standing in March wondering where to start, because you've been moving forward all year.

The hardest part is the first month. January. Setting up the folder, committing to the system. After that, it's maintenance. And maintenance, once you're in the rhythm, doesn't feel like work. It feels like brushing your teeth. You just do it, because not doing it would be weirder.

So here's what I want you to do. Not in March. Not when you're panicking. Right now, whatever month you're reading this.

Create the folder. Physical or digital, doesn't matter. Label it with the current year. Put it somewhere you'll see it. Kitchen counter, desktop, home screen—wherever you naturally look. Then make a deal with yourself: any time you encounter something that might be tax-relevant, you toss it in. No organizing, no categorizing, no thinking. Just toss.

That's it. That's the whole first step. You're not preparing a return. You're not calculating anything. You're just creating one central place where tax stuff lives instead of seventeen scattered places you'll never remember.

Next month—whatever month that is for you—you'll spend thirty minutes sorting what you've collected. The month after that, you'll add a simple projection. You're building the system one month at a time, and by the time December arrives, you won't be starting from scratch. You'll be closing out a process you've been running all year.

And when April comes—when Chris is sitting at his kitchen table surrounded by shoeboxes and panic, when your coworkers are complaining about tax season and extensions and how much they owe—you'll be done. You'll have filed weeks ago, because there was nothing left to do. No scramble. No surprises. No resignation.

Just the quiet confidence that comes from knowing exactly where you stand, because you've been paying attention all along.

That shift—from reactive scramble to proactive routine—doesn't just change how you file taxes. It changes how you think about money entirely.

Because here's what happens when you spend a year tracking quarterly, reconciling monthly, projecting ahead: you stop treating your income like a mystery. You stop being surprised by your own financial life. The anxiety that comes from not knowing—*How much do I actually make? How much will I owe? Can I afford this?*—dissolves, not because the numbers got better, but because you finally know what the numbers are.

And once you know, you can plan.

You can set aside money for a business expense in July because you can see it coming in September. You can decide whether to take on a new client in November based on what that income will actually mean after taxes. You can choose to invest in your business—or yourself—without the gnawing fear that you're spending money the IRS is going to demand back in April.

This is what financial stability actually feels like. Not having more money. Not earning more. Just *knowing* what you have, what you owe, and what's yours to keep.

The proactive taxpayer system doesn't make you rich. It makes you certain. And certainty, it turns out, is worth more than most people realize.

* * *

Let's say you're two years in.

It's February. You've just closed out January's books. You open your quarterly tracker, glance at Q1, and realize you're on pace to owe about $2,800 by April. You've already set aside $2,400. You're $400 short.

Two years ago, this would have been a crisis. A surprise bill. A reason to panic, to pull from savings, to feel like you failed somehow.

Now? It's a data point.

You look at February's projected income. You're expecting about $4,200 this month. You decide to set aside an extra $200 this month and another $200 in March. Problem solved. No drama. No scramble. Just a small course correction based on information you already had.

This is what the system gives you. Not perfection—you're still going to have months where income is high or low, where expenses shift, where estimates need adjusting. But you'll have *visibility*. You'll see the gap while there's still time to close it. You'll make decisions in February instead of discovering problems in April.

And that visibility compounds.

By year three, you'll know your effective tax rate within a percentage point. You'll know which expenses are worth tracking and which ones don't move the needle. You'll know whether you should be making estimated payments or if setting aside monthly is enough. You'll have a sense—a real, grounded sense—of what your financial year looks like before it's even halfway done.

You won't need an accountant to tell you if you're on track. You'll already know.

* * *

Here's the part that surprises people: once you build this system for taxes, you start using the same mindset everywhere else.

You start tracking business revenue the same way—not just what you invoiced, but what actually came in. You start projecting cash flow, not by hoping this month will be better than last month, but by looking at patterns, at what actually happens when you do the work you do.

You start making financial decisions based on data instead of optimism.

And that shift—that move from "I think I'm doing okay" to "I know exactly where I stand"—changes everything. It changes whether you say yes to a project. It changes whether you hire help. It changes whether you feel anxious on Sunday nights or confident.

Because the anxiety was never really about taxes. It was about *not knowing*. It was about living in a fog, where your financial reality was always a few months behind your actual life, where you were constantly guessing and hoping and bracing for bad news.

The proactive system clears the fog. It doesn't make the work easier—you're still running a business, still navigating complexity, still dealing with uncertainty. But it makes *you* steadier. It gives you a foundation. And from that foundation, you can build something sustainable.

* * *

So let's go back to April.

You file your return on a Tuesday morning. It takes twenty minutes, because your accountant already has everything and there are no surprises. You owe $3,100. You've set aside $3,300. You pay the bill, close your laptop, and go back to work.

No drama. No dread. No emotional hangover that lasts through May.

And here's the moment that matters: it's April 20th, and you're sitting across from a friend—a fellow freelancer, someone who's been doing this as long as you have—and they're talking about taxes the way people always do. The stress. The extensions. The shoebox of receipts they still haven't sorted. How much they think they might owe, but they're afraid to find out.

And you realize: you don't feel that way anymore.

You're not special. You're not better at math. You didn't hire a fancy accountant or discover some secret loophole. You just built a system—a simple, repeatable system—and followed it for twelve months.

That's all it took.

And now, when someone asks how you handle taxes, you don't commiserate. You don't join the collective groan. You just say, "I track it as I go. It's really not that bad."

And you mean it.

Because the proactive taxpayer system didn't just change your taxes. It changed your relationship with your own financial life. It gave you agency. It gave you clarity. It gave you the quiet, unshakable confidence that comes from knowing—really knowing—where you stand.

And that confidence doesn't just show up in April.

It shows up every single month, in every decision you make, in the way you sleep at night and the way you open your bank account without flinching.

That's what proactive looks like.

And once you've felt it, you'll never go back.

Also in the Series

Every book in Money Reset stands on its own — read them in any order. If this one was useful, the library continues:

Salary Negotiation Before You Sign

Budgeting for People Who Hate Budgeting

Budgeting From Zero

Budgeting on an Irregular Income

Couples Budgeting

Budgeting After Debt

Budgeting for the Broke Paycheck

Budgeting Without a Spreadsheet

Budgeting for Impulse Spending

Budgeting for a Bigger Life

www.ingramcontent.com/pod-product-compliance
Lightning Source LLC
LaVergne TN
LVHW010728061126
851857LV00014B/1388
* 9 7 8 1 8 0 4 2 8 2 4 7 2 *